Aquaculture in Southeast Asia

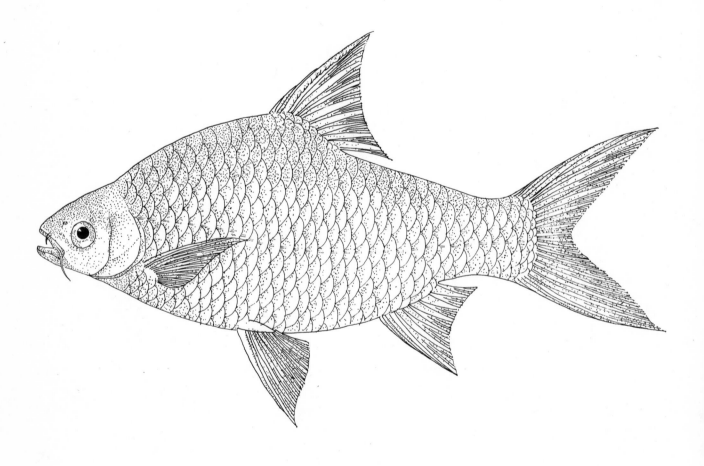

ILLUSTRATION 4.   Puntius carp (Tawes)   *Puntius gonionotus* (Blkr.) (After Arifin)

Aquaculture in Southeast Asia
A Historical Overview

Shao-Wen Ling
Edited by Laura Mumaw

A WASHINGTON SEA GRANT PUBLICATION
in cooperation with the College of Fisheries, University of Washington
Distributed by UNIVERSITY OF WASHINGTON PRESS, Seattle and London

The U.S. Government is authorized to produce and distribute reprints for governmental purposes notwithstanding any copyright notation that may appear hereon.

Copyright © 1977 by the Division of Marine Resources, University of Washington
Printed in the United States of America

Library of Congress Cataloging in Publication Data

Ling, Shao-Wen, 1907-
  Aquaculture in Southeast Asia.

  (A Washington sea grant publication)   (Contribution - College of Fisheries, University of Washington ; no. 465)
  "[Prepared] in cooperation with the College of Fisheries, University of Washington."
  Consists of the author's lectures given at the College of Fisheries, University of Washington, autumn quarters, 1974-1975.
  Bibliography: p.
  1. Aquaculture—Asia, Southeastern—History. I. Washington (State). University. College of Fisheries.
II. Title. III. Series: A Washington sea grant publication (unnumb.)
SH117.S68L56   639'.31   77-3828
ISBN 0-295-95560-0
ISBN 0-295-95563-5 pbk.

Contents

FIGURES AND ILLUSTRATIONS ix

TABLES xi

FOREWORD xiii

ACKNOWLEDGMENTS xv

INTRODUCTION 1

HISTORY OF AQUACULTURE IN SOUTHEAST ASIA 4

SPECIES CULTURED IN SOUTHEAST ASIA 8

COLLECTION AND PRODUCTION OF STOCKING MATERIAL 27

Stocking Material Collected from Natural Sources 27

Stocking Material Produced under Controlled Conditions 29
    Natural spawning 29
    Induced spawning 29
        Nest builders 31
        Adhesive egg-layers 32
        Hormone treatment 33

CULTURING FACILITIES 36

Ponds 36

Lakes and Water Reservoirs 37

Swamps, Marshes, Mangroves 38

Ricefields 38

Pens and Corrals 38

Cages and Baskets 38

AQUACULTURE PRACTICES AND TECHNIQUES: INTRODUCTION 39

Natural Stocking 39
    Trapping-holding-growing ponds 39
    Simple pond operation 39
    Ricefield fish culture 40

Controlled Stocking 40
    Monoculture 40
    Polyculture 40
    Fish culture integrated with aquaculture or animal husbandry 40

TILAPIA CULTURE 41

Common Tilapia Culture Method 42
    Water conditions and pond preparation 42
    Stocking practices 42
    Feed 43
    Harvesting 43

Other Tilapia Culture Methods 43

MILKFISH *(Chanos chanos)* CULTURE 44

History 44

Milkfish Fry 45

Procurement of Stocking Material 45

Food 46
    Filamentous algae 46
    Blue-green benthic algae 46
    Diatoms 46

Pond Characteristics 47

Pond Preparation 47

Maintenance of Water Conditions 49

Fish Stocking and Stock Manipulation 50

Production and Maintenance of Food 50
    Single-size stocking 50
    Multiple-size stocking 51

Control of Pests and Predators 52

Harvesting 53

Transportation to Market 54

Problems 55

WALKING CATFISH *(Clarias batrachus)* CULTURE 56

Water Conditions and Pond Preparation 57

Stocking Material and Practices 57

Feed 58

SNAKEHEAD *(Ophicephalus* spp.) CULTURE 60

Water Conditions and Pond Preparation 61

Stocking Material and Practices 61

Grow-out Operation 62

FRESHWATER EEL *(Anguilla japonica)* CULTURE 65

Stocking 66

Ponds 67

Feed 67

Harvesting 68

Transportation to Market 68

PEN CULTURE 70

CAGE CULTURE 72

RICEFIELD FISH CULTURE 75

POLYCULTURE 78

Stocking Material 79

Ponds 80

Stocking Methods 81

Feed 81

Harvesting 83

COMBINATION POLYCULTURE 88

CRUSTACEAN CULTURE 90

Marine Shrimp 90
   Natural stocking 90
   Controlled stocking 91

Freshwater Prawns 94
   Some historical notes 94
   Problems concerning reproduction—mating and breeding 94

   Problems of larval survival 95
   Problems concerning larval food and feeding 95
Current Status of Prawn Culture in Southeast Asia 96

Crab Culture 97

OUTLOOK FOR THE FUTURE 99

APPENDIX 103

GLOSSARY 105

REFERENCES 107

Figures and Illustrations

Illustrations by the Author

1. Milkfish . . . . *Chanos chanos* (Forskal) (After H. C. Yang) . . . . 9 and 44

2. Tilapia . . . . *Tilapia mossambica* (Peters) . . . . 17 and 41

3. Common carp . . . . *Cyprinus carpio* L. (After Arifin) . . . . 18 and 73

4. Puntius carp (Tawes) . . . . . . *Puntius gonionotus* (Blkr.) (After Arifin) . . . . 18 and ii

5. Grass carp . . . . *Ctenopharyngodon idellus* (Cuvier and Valenciennes)
(After H. C. Yang) . . . . 19 and 82

6. Silver carp . . . . *Hypophthalmichthys molitrix* (Cuvier and Valenciennes)
(After H. C. Yang) . . . . 20 and 100

7. Bighead carp . . . . *Aristichthys nobilis* (Richardson) (After H. C. Yang) . . . . . . 20 and 33

8. Clarias catfish . . . . *Clarias batrachus* (L.) (After Arifin) . . . . 21 and 56

9. Snakehead fish . . . . *Ophicephalus striatus* Bl. (After Arifin) . . . . 21 and 60

10. Giant gourami . . . . *Osphronemus goramy* Lac. . . . . 22 and 30

11. Siamese gourami . . . . *Trichogaster pectoralis* Regan (After Arifin) . . . . 22 and 76

Figures

1. Sketch map of Southeast Asia 5

2. Bamboo nest frame for giant gourami 31

3. Layout of typical milkfish pond in Taiwan (after Chen, 1952). 48

4. Layout of typical snakehead pond 63

5. A Interrelationship between the major groups of fish-food biota in a pond 79

   B Interrelationship between fish of different food habits stocked in the same pond 79

Tables

1. Estimates of annual aquaculture production worldwide and in Asia and the Far East, 1972 2

2. Estimates of annual production through aquaculture in 15 Asian countries, 1972. 3

3. Principal species being cultured or having high potential for culturing in Southeast Asia 10

4. Annual milkfish production in Southeast Asia 46

5. Benthic algal production in a 1-hectare milkfish pond (Taiwan) 51

6. Daily food requirements and growth rate of milkfish 51

7. Weight increase and corresponding food demand of milkfish stocked in multiple sizes (Taiwan) 51

8. Projected annual profit and loss statement for a 1-hectare milkfish pond (Taiwan, 1973) 54

9. Stocking characteristics and corresponding culture time for catfish (Thailand) 57

10. Projected profit and loss statement per crop for an average Clarias catfish pond (Thailand, 1973) 59

11. Projected annual profit and loss statement for an average snakehead pond (Taiwan, 1973) 64

12. Total area of commercial eel farms for selected years (Taiwan, after 1952) 65

13. Cost of elvers (Taiwan, after 1952) 66

14. Projected annual profit and loss statement for a 1-hectare eel farm (Taiwan, 1973) 68

15. Stocking rates for cage cultured *Pangasius* (Cambodia) 74

16. Projected annual profit and loss statement for a 1-hectare polyculture fish pond (Taiwan, 1974) 84

17. Annual wet weight production and $E\beta$ values of standing crops of biotic constituents in two types of impoundments (Taiwan, 1970) 85

18. Species composition of fish populations harvested from two types of impoundments (1 year) 86

19. Organic material commonly used as fertilizer in polyculture ponds in Southeast Asia (1 year) 87

Foreword

Although I myself did not personally meet Dr. Shao-Wen Ling until 1974 when I attended the 5th Annual World Mariculture Society Meeting in Charleston, South Carolina, I had long been familiar with his work. His tremendous contributions to the scientific community have earned him worldwide recognition and he is regarded as a "giant" in the field of aquaculture.

Dr. Ling is also known among his colleagues as the "father" of freshwater prawn farming, a new industry in many countries throughout the world. He was the first person successfully to rear the Malaysian prawn *(Macrobrachium rosenbergii)* from egg to adult under controlled conditions. He is also considered a world authority on the culture of warmwater fishes.

Dr. Ling's keynote address at the 5th Annual World Mariculture Society Meeting not only revealed his vast knowledge of aquaculture but also reflected his deep personal concern with feeding the people of the world. We at the College of Fisheries at the University of Washington subsequently invited him that same year to share his knowledge with us by teaching a special class on "Aquaculture in Southeast Asia." This class was so well received that Dr. Ling was asked to teach the class the following year (1975), and he was honored by being awarded a Walker-Ames Professorship, established "... to guarantee the state of Washington the scholarly and educational services of the most distinguished minds available to this and other countries."

Dr. Ling's approach to lecturing is an art in itself. As he teaches, he not only captures the student's interest but also instills an enthusiasm for the subject that is truly inspirational. He takes one through the social, political, economic, and biological aspects of aquatic husbandry in Asia, giving the course an interdisciplinary character.

His lectures are a marvelous blend of love and enthusiasm for the subject coupled with a love and concern for the students. He truly believes in the Chinese custom—that the students are the "children" of the professor and their children are the professor's "grandchildren."

From this warm, modest man, emanates an infectious enthusiasm, enveloping all those around him. This warmth and graciousness are evident also in his wife, Jeannette Ling. Her assistance, encouragement, and companionship throughout his career have no doubt contributed greatly to his work.

Dr. Ling was born in Changchow, Fukien, China in 1907. He received both his bachelor's and master's degree from Yeching University in his native China and his Ph.D. from Cornell University in the United States. He also holds several honorary degrees. He has served as Associate Professor of Biology at Amoy University, Professor of Biology at Shantung University, Professor and Head of the Biology Department of the National Kweiyang Medical College and the National Defense Medical College at Kweiyang, China.

Following World War II, Dr. Ling's professional emphasis shifted to the field of aquaculture. He served as Director of the Chinese National Fisheries Research Institute, Shanghai, China, and in 1949 he was appointed by the Food and Agriculture Organization of the United Nations (FAO) as a Regional Officer. In 1951 he became a Technical Assistance Expert and served in Thailand, Ceylon (Sri Lanka), and Malaysia until 1965. From 1965 to 1972, Dr. Ling served as FAO Regional Fish Culturist for Asia and the Far East.

Presently, Dr. Ling serves as Adjunct Professor of Aquaculture at the School of Marine and Atmospheric Sciences at the University of Miami. Although technically retired as a Regional Fish Culturist, he is far from "retired" since he remains deeply involved in the training, planning, and development of warm-water fish and prawn culture.

We are indeed honored to be able to publish these lectures by Dr. Ling, and we are sure that the reader will be as delighted as we are with the cover and text illustrations, which Dr. Ling himself has drawn.

Dr. Kenneth K. Chew
Professor of Fisheries
University of Washington
Seattle, Washington

January 1977

Acknowledgments

"Give a person a fish and he will have food for a day; teach him to grow fish and he will have food for a lifetime." So goes an old Chinese saying. Application of this wisdom on a worldwide scale could well assist in producing food for the hungry millions.

A great deal of practical knowledge in fish farming has been accumulated through centuries of down-to-earth experience in Asia and the Far East. To help spread the principles and philosophy of such valuable practices has long been my ambition. The opportunity for me to do so was made possible through the support and assistance of my colleagues and friends at the University of Washington. To them I owe much appreciation and thanks.

Special thanks are due to Dean Douglas G. Chapman and Professor Kenneth K. Chew of the University's College of Fisheries and to Dr. Stanley R. Murphy, Director of the Division of Marine Resources. Their kind efforts enabled me to serve as Visiting Professor to present a series of lectures on "The Status and Problems of Aquaculture in Southeast Asian Countries" to students in the College of Fisheries during Autumn Quarter 1974 and again in Autumn Quarter 1975. The material used in this series of lectures was edited into this present report.

To the Graduate School of the University of Washington, I wish to extend thanks for honoring me with the award of the prestigious Walker-Ames Professorship for Autumn Quarter 1975. Under this award, I was given the opportunity to deliver a series of three public lectures on the subject of aquaculture. Some of the material used in this series of lectures has been incorporated into this publication.

My deep appreciation is due to Washington Sea Grant, the Division of Marine Resources, and the College of Fisheries, at the University of Washington for providing the necessary financial support and other valuable assistance for having my lecture series edited and published in its present form.

To Ms. Laura Mumaw, I wish to express appreciation and thanks for handling the difficult task of recording, transcribing, organizing, and editing my lectures so patiently and satisfactorily.

To Mr. T. P. Chen and Mr. H. S. Yang, Taiwan, I extend thanks for permission to copy some of the fish drawings used in their publication *Common Food Fish of Taiwan*, published by J.C.R.R., Taiwan, 1971. Appreciation and thanks are also due to Ms. BIEN Po-chung, J.C.R.R., Taiwan, for her kind assistance in the preparation of many of the fish drawings.

Most important of all, it was the youthful inspiration, persistent urging, and cooperation of Dr. Kenneth K. Chew that enabled this piece of work to be initiated and to progress to its present form. Hearty thanks to you, Ken!

1 Introduction[1]

Fisheries is one of the youngest and often one of the least appreciated sciences in the world. Yet over half of the world's population depends on fish as its principal source of animal protein.

If we compare conditions in this country to those elsewhere, we begin to understand that our "food crisis" is relatively minor. In some of the developing countries, people seldom know whether they will have anything at all to eat the next day. There is a corresponding difference in the development of aquaculture between those countries and this one. The United States has made excellent progress in such specialized areas as salmon, trout, bass, and catfish culture. In many other areas, especially in cheap, staple fish production, it has barely begun.

In China we have an old saying: "If you give a person a fish, he will have food for one day; but if you teach him to raise fish, he will have food for a lifetime." I hope to bring a message from the East: information on what people there are doing in the field of aquaculture (especially in areas not yet developed here), the history of aquaculture since it began in China some 4,000 years ago, how it progressed, what its present status is, and what the trends and problems of development are. From this message it is possible to derive certain lessons. There are many failures people in the East have committed that Americans can avoid. There are many good cultural techniques, which although not yet fully studied scientifically, may open up new avenues of development and provide challenges for research and experimentation.

In the field of aquaculture, emphasis is placed on the production of fish, shrimps, molluscs, seaweeds, and other aquatic organisms. There are opportunities to engage in practical research, to develop an industry, to help one's country, or, if one has the missionary spirit, to help people of other countries. I have met many volunteer fisheries workers over the past 15 years; many had majored in history, English, political science, or economics. Learning of the poor living conditions and virtual starvation of the peoples in Asia and Africa, they decided to devote their time and talent to helping those people. They were told that fish culture is one of the most effective food-producing practices, and so they enrolled themselves in a volunteer organization where they received short course training in fisheries. They were young, idealistic, and full of enthusiasm, and they thought that a few weeks of training in the United States would enable them to help the "ignorant" regions of the world. They were quite surprised when they arrived at their destinations and found that people there were not so ignorant after all, although they did have very different socioeconomic backgrounds and living standards.

The volunteers were accustomed to the high standard of living in the United States. They had seen the elaborately constructed hatcheries and ponds and the expensive methods used to culture fish there. A $1 million fish hatchery may be commonplace in the United States, but in some of the developing countries $1 million may represent the entire budget for all fisheries work for one year. That one hatchery would require $1 million is incomprehensible to many Southeast Asians. People in developing countries need help, but help cannot be delivered effectively without adequate preparation and planning. When we want to help the people of the so-called developing countries, we must understand the socioeconomic conditions under which they live.

What are some of the important roles played by aquaculture in Southeast Asia today?

Aquaculture plays a tremendous role in national development as a source of food for the common man. While soybean is the staple plant protein of most Southeast Asians, fish is their staple animal protein. The av-

1. Contribution No. 465, College of Fisheries, University of Washington.

erage per capita consumption of fish in Southeast Asia is 25-30 pounds, more than twice the United States average of 10-12 pounds. The Japanese consume 60-70 pounds of fish per person per year. Seventy-five percent of the fish consumed in Southeast Asia are taken from wild stocks; the remaining 25% are produced by aquaculture.

Some expensive fish are cultured for export as luxury items, bringing in much-needed foreign exchange. This foreign exchange helps to stabilize the economies of many of the Southeast Asian countries. Aquaculture is responsible for the tremendous production of ornamental and aquarium fish exported from Southeast Asia to the United States and Europe every year. This business continues to grow at a fantastic rate.

Bait fish are cultured for the commercial fishermen. Natural production of bait has declined markedly in the last 10-15 years, while high-seas fishing is still on the increase. Milkfish, which grow rapidly and are slender and shiny when young, have proven to be excellent bait for chumming such fish as tuna. Bait fish farms are also found in the United States, but these serve primarily sportsmen (e.g. Arkansas minnow farms).

Aquaculture is also a good means of utilizing human and animal waste as fertilizer or directly as feed for fish. Aquaculture has made possible the utilization of previously wasted "trash" fish making up 60-70% of the fish captured in trawl fisheries in Southeast Asia. These fish are not eaten, but can be used in the culture of carnivorous fish grown for human consumption. The culture of the carnivorous "walking catfish" (Clarias spp.), extensively developed in Thailand, Indonesia, and the Philippines, is an excellent example.

Aquaculture helps to control water pollution and eutrophication[2] when the proper species of fish are stocked in lakes, reservoirs, and other bodies of water. Eutrophication and other types of water pollution precipitated by excess organic wastes seldom occur where

proper stocking of macrophyte and plankton-feeding fish has taken place.

Aquaculture has also served to reclaim largely unproductive land. Thousands of hectares of mangrove swamps, tidal flats, lowlands, and flood plains have been converted into productive fish ponds every year. Unfortunately, many of these converted areas will in the near future be used for agricultural or industrial purposes. Since we need more food, and usable lands are becoming scarce, we must extend our efforts in reclaiming "wastelands."

Aquaculture has become increasingly important in the production of a number of commercially useful goods. Pearls can now be grown in a variety of colors and shapes. Algae is cultivated for food and as a source of agar, carrageenin, and alginic acid, all marine extractives used extensively in food, cosmetic, and textile industries.

Aquaculture offers many opportunities for employment to Southeast Asians. It has been roughly estimated that 500,000 hectares are presently being used for aquaculture in Southeast Asia. On the average, one person can manage 2-4 hectares. This means that 100-200,000 people are currently employed in aquaculture-related endeavors. Most of the present operations are labor-in-

TABLE 1.

ESTIMATES OF ANNUAL AQUACULTURE PRODUCTION WORLDWIDE AND IN ASIA AND THE FAR EAST, 1972

ITEM	WORLD PRODUCTION (metric tons)	ASIA, FAR EAST PRODUCTION (metric tons)
Finfish	3,657,373	3,249,522
Crustaceans (crab, shrimps, prawns)	14,298	14,248
Molluscs	966,400	401,950
Edible seaweed	474,500	474,500
TOTAL	5,112,571	4,140,220

Source: Primarily reports from the UN Food and Agricultural Organization.

---

2. For a definition of eutrophication and other unfamiliar terms in this book, consult glossary, p. 104.

tensive, and energy and economic crises make it probable that they will remain so for quite some time. It has been conservatively estimated that 5 million hectares of land with high aquaculture potential remain undeveloped. Using the same manpower requirement (4 hectares/person), aquaculture could create a total of 1.25 million more jobs.

TABLE 2.

ESTIMATES OF ANNUAL PRODUCTION THROUGH AQUACULTURE IN 15 ASIAN COUNTRIES, 1972

COUNTRY	FINFISH PRODUCTION (metric tons)	CRUSTACEAN PRODUCTION— CRABS, SHRIMP, PRAWNS (metric tons)	MOLLUSC PRODUCTION (metric tons)			EDIBLE SEAWEED PRODUCTION (metric)	TOTAL
			OYSTERS	MUSSELS	CLAMS, COCKLES		
Burma	1,493						1,493
Cambodia	5,000						5,000
China (Mainland)	2,240,000					100,000A	2,340,000
Hongkong	690		5,000C				5,690
India	480,000	3,800					483,800
Indonesia	141,075	3,328					144,403
Japan	85,000	250	194,600		10,000	357,000	646,850
Korea	40		45,700	16,800	16,800	16,000	95,340
Malaysia	25,648	250			28,600		54,498
Philippines	94,573	2,500	6,000B				103,073
Singapore	554	120					674
South Vietnam	16,500	500	2,000B				19,000
Sri Lanka (Ceylon)	15,000						15,000
Taiwan (China)	56,185	800B	13,000B		3,450B	1,500B	74,935
Thailand	87,764	2,500	5,000B	40,000B	15,000D		150,264
TOTAL	3,249,522	14,048	271,300	56,800	73,850	474,500	4,140,020

Source: Reports from the UN Food and Agricultural Organization, with exceptions noted.
A. Very rough estimate.
B. Ling's estimate.
C. Includes approximately 1,000 metric tons produced by other Southeast Asian countries.
D. With shell—Ling's estimate.

2 History of Aquaculture in Southeast Asia

Aquaculture had its cradle in Asia. It developed there some four thousand years ago in harmony with a traditional rural-agrarian economy, and it is now heading towards some fascinating developments. We shall examine aquaculture in the Southeast Asian region, including Indonesia, the Philippines, Malaysia, Singapore, Vietnam, Cambodia, Thailand, Burma, and the southern China coast to Taiwan (Figure 1). I shall try to give a basic understanding of fish culture in Southeast Asia by explaining the concepts and philosophy behind many of the practices. It is impossible, however, to prescribe a formula of success, for fish culture is still an art, striving to become a technology. Even the author of a Chinese cookbook, following his own recipe, cannot produce a dish with exactly the same results each time. With an understanding of the concepts underlying Eastern fish culture, it is possible to modify the particulars to suit specific conditions. However, trying to duplicate Eastern ways entirely will not prove successful.

Let us first look at the history of aquaculture in Asia and the Far East since its beginning over thirty-five hundred years ago. In Asia and the Far East, especially China, fish is regarded as the best kind of food, highly valued by every family. From time immemorial, if a person wanted to please someone, he gave him a fish. Fish was served and still is served at all festivals, social functions, family celebrations, and religious ceremonies. In Chinese, the word "fish" sounds exactly like the word "surplus." It carries the meaning that we are blessed with bounty for this year and all the years to come. In many Chinese paintings, one sees a fish jumping over a wave, and the fish happens to be a carp. This jumping carp symbolizes success, a jump to a higher level—the fish is ascending to the dragon's gate. Fish occupy such a high position in the tradition of Chinese history that fish culture developed in China widely and extensively.

Fish culture is first noted in Chinese records before the development of paper over thirty-five hundred years ago. In these ancient times, one of the ways to decide important matters was to ask instruction from "Heaven." Matters to be decided were inscribed on scapular bones of large domestic animals or on turtle shells which were baked on fire in an altar during a special ceremony until they cracked, and the resulting pattern of the inscriptions on the cracked pieces was "read by priests" or special officials as messages or instructions from "Heaven." Such bones and shells are known as "oracle bones." Many of these oracle bones and shell fragments bear mention of favorable times for planting or harvesting fish.

Fish culture became a popular practice in China around 1000 B.C.; at this time only the common carp, *Cyprinus carpio,* was cultured. We can only speculate as to why people began culturing fish so long ago. It is said that in those times if an emperor desired fish, even in the dead of winter, he had to have it. His prime ministers learned that to keep their heads they had to have a supply of live fish year-round. This may have induced many of them to maintain gardens beautified by fish ponds. In the dead of winter, the ice covering the pond could be broken, hot water poured through the hole, and the fish that congregated in the warm spot captured for use.

The technique of keeping fish in a pond is supposed to have originated with fishermen who kept their surplus catch alive temporarily in baskets submerged in rivers or small bodies of water created by damming one side of a river bed. Gradually these fishermen learned that if the holding area was well protected and if they supplied the captive fish with food, they would grow. Another possibility is that aquaculture stems from the ancient practice of trapping fish. At certain times of the year when the water level of rivers and streams rose,

Figure 1.

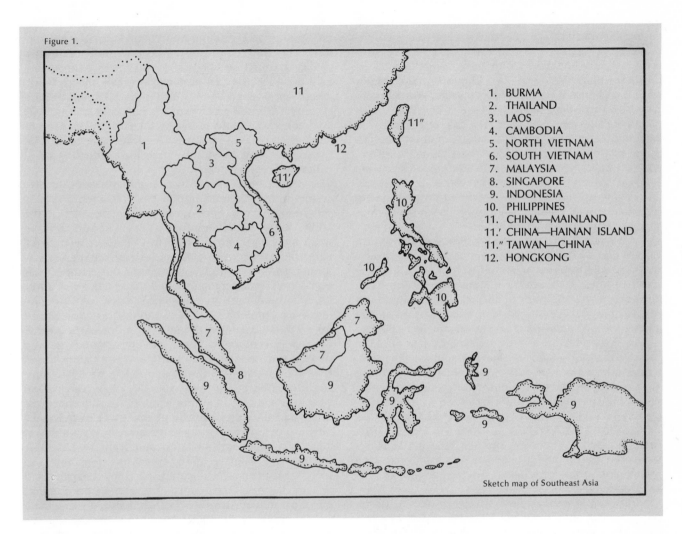

1. BURMA
2. THAILAND
3. LAOS
4. CAMBODIA
5. NORTH VIETNAM
6. SOUTH VIETNAM
7. MALAYSIA
8. SINGAPORE
9. INDONESIA
10. PHILIPPINES
11. CHINA—MAINLAND
11.' CHINA—HAINAN ISLAND
11." TAIWAN—CHINA
12. HONGKONG

Sketch map of Southeast Asia

people would (and still do) build trapping ponds alongside the banks. Many kinds and sizes of fish entered the trapping ponds; large ones were harvested while young, smaller ones were left behind. This simple trapping operation was steadily improved and gradually developed from trapping-holding to trapping-holding-growing practices, and finally into culture operations when people learned how to collect or produce fry and fingerlings for stocking.

In other countries of Southeast Asia, aquaculture also developed gradually over hundreds of years, probably from simple trapping, to trapping-holding, to trapping-holding-growing, and finally into complete husbandry practices. Most Southeast Asian countries harbored large numbers of Chinese immigrants early in their history who carried with them something to remember their old home by. Common carp, highly prized, and able to tolerate long voyages in small containers, were often brought. These immigrants introduced the Chinese method of carp culture and inspired local people to take up fish farming. Common carp became an important fish in Southeast Asian countries, and fish culture practices were either copied from the Chinese directly or based on their methods. Gradually the established methods of Chinese carp culture were extended and modified to suit the culture of indigenous species of the respective countries.

Around 500 B.C. the famous Chinese classic on fish culture was written by Fan Lee,[3] a popular, able politician and administrator, who trained himself to become a fish culturist. He was so successful that he was often invited by kings and lords of ancient Chinese kingdoms to give them advice. In his treatise, Fan Lee notes that among the five good ways of making a living, aquahusbandry is the first. It was then, in 500 B.C., that the term "aquahusbandry" was first used to depict the technology of fish culture. Some of the explanations Fan Lee gives for his techniques do not make modern scientific sense, but the techniques are based on valid, well-accepted biological principles. Fan Lee begins by describing the construction of a fish pond. He gives the preferred size of the pond and suggests that small islands be constructed inside it. The fish, swimming around and around the islands, will feel as though they are swimming in big lakes and rivers.

Fan Lee describes how to spawn the fish—the selection of mature male and female brood stock—in a time when many peoples still believed that fish arose spontaneously from decaying aquatic weeds. He explains how to control fish population, and thus prevent stunting. At that time people believed that some of the

3. See Appendix.

fish actually did grow large but flew away, carried off by evil spirits. Fan Lee prescribed the addition of a few turtles to the pond as "heavenly guardians." These turtles actually thinned out the fish population by eating some of the young. Fan Lee also explains why the common carp is an excellent fish for culturing: (1) common carp is tasty; (2) common carp is not cannibalistic; (3) common carp grows rapidly, is hardy, and easy to handle; and (4) common carp is inexpensive to culture. These principles are still the basis for conducting aquaculture successfully today.

500 B.C. to 500 A.D. was a golden period for the culture of the common carp in China. In about 618 A.D. the Tang Dynasty was founded. It happened that the family name of the Emperor was Lee. The sound of the word meaning common carp in Chinese is also "lee." Since the name "Lee" itself was sacred, the idea of culturing "lee" in ponds, then catching and eating it, was outrageous and sacrilegious, and the practice was absolutely forbidden. People began to search for fish to replace the common carp in culturing. The crisis turned out to be a blessing in disguise. From the earliest times Chinese fish culture had been centered around one kind of fish and one kind of practice—carp monoculture. Now four additional fish were found to be suitable for culturing. These four fish were the grass carp, silver carp, bighead carp, and mud carp. Grass carp specialize in eating submerged aquatic plants; silver carp actively devour phytoplankton; the bighead carp is an efficient zooplankton feeder; and the mud carp is a benthic feeder. The Chinese grew these fish together, and without realizing its significance, they developed a system of polyculture which they carried on as traditional practice for another thirteen hundred years. Forty to fifty years ago biologists began to study and analyze the scientific basis of polyculture in China, and only then was it introduced to the Western world. In some areas in Southeast Asia polyculture has been successfully integrated with other agricultural and animal husbandry practices such as chicken or duck raising, hog rearing, vegetable gardening, and silkworm production.

Brackish-water culture began much later than freshwater culture in Southeast Asia. It is believed to have started around 1400 A.D. in Indonesia with the culture of milkfish. Milkfish is still the main species cultured in the brackish water of Southeast Asia, although the culture of mullet, *Mugil cephalus,* has also been practiced, usually in combination with other fish. The culture of crustaceans, molluscs, and algae is of rather recent introduction.

The traditional systems of aquaculture were practiced in China by the common man without help from the government for years. It was only at the beginning of the 20th century that the government felt that new concepts and ideas should be applied to the field. At that time modern sciences had already been introduced into China, and young students and scholars were sent abroad to study biology. Nobody was trained specifically in fisheries, but some of the young biologists took an interest in it and became fisheries biologists and fish culturists. In those days most of the biology teachers in China were trained in foreign countries, and were taught using foreign textbooks and foreign organisms as examples. In the early 1920s a group of progressive young biologists began to study Chinese animals and plants and write Chinese biology textbooks. Although these efforts were devoted mainly to natural studies, fisheries as a subject was beginning to receive attention, and some of the young scientists tried to interpret the traditional aquaculture operations on a scientific basis, Many of the old fish masters were illiterate, but they possessed invaluable practical experience and skill. By observing weather conditions, the color of pond water, or the movement and behavior of fish, they could determine reasonably accurately the water quality of the pond and the health of the fish. They could detect important deviations from the norm, and knew how to correct or prevent such undesirable happenings without the aid of expensive equipment. Asian scientists gradually began to apply their knowledge of biological and physical principles to the practices of the old masters. It was at this time that fish polyculture became known to the world.

Before World War II, most scientific fisheries work involved the survey and interpretation of existing practices. With the realization of the potential of aquaculture to produce cheap protein food, efforts began to pour into fish culture, and experiments were initiated to improve and refine existing practices. It was not until the early 1950s that serious efforts were made to produce quality "seed," or stocking material. Traditionally, "fry seed" of the major carps was collected from natural habitats. In 1955 the technique of using hormones (e.g. human chorionic gonadotropine, fish pituitary gland extract) to induce spawning provided a major breakthrough. Many fish that could not be spawned previously could now be induced to reproduce in simple hatcheries under controlled conditions, resulting in successful mass production of quality fish seed of many of the important cultivable species. Recently, new problems have arisen in Southeast Asian aquaculture. Traditional practices had been sufficient to satisfy the needs of a simple, rural-agrarian mode of life, but in this day of technology they are not good enough. Change is necessary, but how much, and how fast?

3 Species Cultured in Southeast Asia

The countries and territories we will consider as Southeast Asia possess tropical climates with similar rainfall patterns and similar flora and fauna. Coconuts, bananas, and other tropical fruits are abundant; everywhere are streams and running waters full of harvestable fish. The people of this rich region developed fish culture so they might have highly prized fish easily available at any time. Many forms of religion are found in this area; some forbid the consumption of beef, others ban pork or chicken, but almost everyone is allowed to eat fish. The great love Southeast Asians have for fish is an important factor in aquaculture development there. The fish occurring throughout this region are more or less the same, but each country has developed the culture of fish most familiar within its borders.

Burma possesses fish native to both the Indian subcontinent and Southeast Asia. Many species of Indian and Chinese carp are cultured there.

Thailand is noted for the culture of both the highly edible Siamese river catfish (*Pangasius* spp.) and the walking, or swamp catfish (*Clarias* spp.). The Siamese gourami is also cultured as a desirable food fish. Along the coastal areas, the Thais are noted for their traditional shrimp farming. Mussel culture is thriving in the Gulf of Thailand, and the harvest is so abundant that there is often more than enough for human consumption, and the surplus is often used as duck or animal feed.

In landlocked Laos, communication is difficult, and ways of living remain simple. The main source of fish are swamps, paddyfields, and the mighty Mekong River and its tributaries. Freshwater fish culture has begun only recently; ponds are few in number and small in size. The principal species cultured in Laos are the common carp and the tilapia; recently Chinese carp have been imported for culture.

Cambodia is known for its huge inland freshwater lake, part of the Mekong River system. This lake produces 40% of the fish the Cambodians consume. Fish culture in floating baskets and cages is practiced extensively along the shores of the large canal connecting this lake and the Mekong River. Other types of fish culture remain underdeveloped.

North and South Vietnam possess rich fresh, brackish, and marine water resources. Major carp are cultured according to practices varying little from traditional Chinese carp culture. Hundreds of hectares of ricefields and brackish-water areas along the coast are converted during the 4 to 5 months of dry season into shrimp ponds when the water salinity is high. Unfortunately, the progress of many developmental fish culture projects has been severely hampered by continuous political and military unrest since World War II.

Malaysia is famous as the birthplace of *Macrobrachium* culture. Ricefield fish culture is widely practiced there using the Siamese gourami. Singapore, a small island south of Malaysia, has converted many mangrove areas along the coast into rich shrimp ponds.

Indonesia is noted as the origin of milkfish culture, centered in Java. It is supposed to have been started as a means of obtaining food by exiles banished to inhospitable jungles in outlying regions. Freshwater fish culture has also been extensively developed, including the culture of the giant gourami (for whom spawning nests are constructed) and many varieties of carp and native fish. Chinese methods of polyculture have also been applied to local species.

Large areas in the Philippines are also devoted to milkfish culture. Recently, milkfish culture in corrals or pens within lagoons has been successfully developed.

Taiwan, one of the three major producers of milkfish along with the Philippines and Indonesia, boasts the greatest per acre harvest, although it farms the smallest acreage and must contend with three winter months during which the milkfish cannot grow. The high yields are associated primarily with good managerial practices. Taiwan is credited for her success in pioneering work on the induced spawning and production of fry and fingerlings of the gray mullet and completion of life history and production of postlarvae of several important culturable penaeid shrimp. Taiwan is also famous for her extensive oyster farming and well-developed polyculture systems, including polyculture of fish integrated with duck or other agricultural and animal husbandry operations. Shrimp culture is practiced either in combination with milkfish or alone. Eel culture has been successfully developed within a short period of less than 20 years. Although slightly outside the tropical region proper, Taiwan is important as a source of information about fish culture practices in southern mainland China.

Hongkong has long served as an international nursery and trading center for fish fry. Until about 20 years ago, Chinese major carp could not be spawned successfully outside Chinese waters, and fry produced in their natural habitats in China were collected and transported to Hongkong for rearing fo fingerling size and then sent to Southeast Asian countries for culturing. Now since these fish can be induced to spawn with pituitary hormone treatment and all these countries are able to produce fingerlings locally, that service has considerably decreased in importance. Polyculture of Chinese fish with the mullet (Mugil) is widely practiced. Hongkong fish farmers specialize in sending their fish to market alive.

As already mentioned, fish culture has a long history in Southeast Asia, and every country has experimented with many kinds of fish, crustaceans, molluscs, and seaweeds. The list given on the following pages includes those major species that people have found worth culturing and those that have high potential for development. A few words about how these organisms were selected for culture may be of interest. What are the principal criteria used for the selection of culturable species by people of many different social and economic backgrounds?

1) The organism must be not only edible, but tasty; 2) it must be popular, with a good market value; 3) the organism must be easy to handle and should be able to tolerate fluctuations in a wide range of environmental conditions; 4) the organism should be capable of growing rapidly to market size; 5) an adequate supply of fry or fingerlings must be steadily and readily available; 6) it should be possible to culture the organism with a minimum of input in the form of time, labor, feed, and other costs. Noncarnivorous fish are highly economical; those fish that can utilize natural production of a pond are the most desired. Carnivorous species can be raised at a profit if the people are willing to pay high prices for them; they then become a luxury item rather than a staple food.

I would like to express caution here. A fish that is well liked in one country may not be readily acceptable elsewhere. Most fish in Table 3 are highly esteemed in Southeast Asia, but some of them may not be popular among most Americans. Fish, as well as systems successfully used in one country, must be given careful consideration before being introduced into another.

Comments on Individual Families

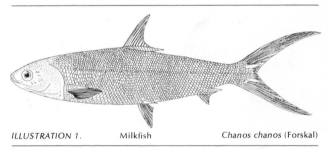

ILLUSTRATION 1.   Milkfish   Chanos chanos (Forskal)

CHANOS CHANOS is the famous milkfish. It is a marine fish, but has been cultured in both brackish and fresh water. This fish is primarily cultured alone, but may be used in combination with other freshwater fishes. It is herbivorous, feeding mainly on blue-green algae and diatoms, especially those growing as the algal mat at the bottom of a pond. Milkfish are usually har-

TABLE 3.

PRINCIPAL SPECIES OF FINFISH, SHELLFISH, AND SEAWEEDS BEING CULTURED
OR HAVING HIGH POTENTIAL FOR CULTURING IN SOUTHEAST ASIAN REGION[A]

SCIENTIFIC AND COMMON NAME	FAMILY	COUNTRY WHERE CULTURED	EXTENT OF DEVELOPMENT	ENVIRONMENT[B]
FINFISH				
Chanos chanos Milkfish	Chanidae	Indonesia	very extensive	F & S
		Malaysia	small scale	S
		Philippines	very extensive	F & S
		Taiwan	very extensive	S
		Thailand	small scale	S
		Vietnam	small scale	S
Anguilla japonica and *Anguilla* spp. Freshwater eel	Anguillidae	Indonesia	experimental	F
		Malaysia	experimental	F
		Philippines	experimental	F
		Singapore	experimental	F & S
		Taiwan	extensive	F & S
		Vietnam	experimental	F
Mugil cephalus and *Mugil* spp. Grey mullet	Mugillidae	Hongkong	extensive	F & S
		Indonesia	experimental	F & S
		Malaysia	experimental	F & S
		Philippines	experimental	F & S
		Singapore	experimental	F & S
		Taiwan	very extensive	F & S
		Vietnam	moderate	F & S
Lates calcarifer Cockup	Latidae	Indonesia	experimental	F
		Malaysia	experimental	F
		Singapore	experimental	F
		Thailand	small scale	F
		Vietnam	experimental	F
Epinephelus spp. Grouper	Serranidae	Hongkong	experimental	S
		Indonesia	experimental	S
		Singapore	experimental	S
		Thailand	experimental	S
		Vietnam	experimental	S
Mylio macrocephalus and *Mylio* spp. Porgy	Sparidae	Hongkong	experimental	S

Sources: Ling, 1972 and 1973; Hora and Pillay, 1962.
A. Comments on many of these species may be found immediately following this table.
B. Environment: F = fresh water; S = salt water or brackish water

TABLE 3. *(continued)*

PRINCIPAL SPECIES OF FINFISH, SHELLFISH, AND SEAWEEDS BEING CULTURED OR HAVING HIGH POTENTIAL FOR CULTURING IN SOUTHEAST ASIAN REGION[A]

SCIENTIFIC AND COMMON NAME	FAMILY	COUNTRY WHERE CULTURED	EXTENT OF DEVELOPMENT	ENVIRONMENT[B]
Chrysophrys major Sea bream	Sparidae	Hongkong	experimental	S
Tilapia mossambica Tilapia	Cichlidae	All countries	moderate to extensive	F & S
Tilapia nilotica	Cichlidae	Taiwan	extensive	F & S
		Thailand	moderate	F & S
Plecoglossus altivelis Sweetfish, Ayu	Plecoglossidae	Taiwan	experimental	F
Cyprinus carpio Common carp	Cyprinidae	All countries	moderate to very extensive	F
Carassius auratus Goldfish (wild)	Cyprinidae	Hongkong	moderate	F
		Indonesia	small scale	F
		Taiwan	extensive	F
		Thailand	moderate	F
		Vietnam	moderate	F
Carassius carassius Crucian carp	Cyprinidae	Indonesia	small scale	F
		Taiwan	moderate	F
Puntius gonionotus and *Puntius* spp. Puntius carp	Cyprinidae	Indonesia	very extensive	F
		Malaysia	extensive	F
		Philippines	moderate	F
		Thailand	extensive	F
		Vietnam	moderate	F
Labeo rohita Rohu	Cyprinidae	Burma	moderate	F
		Malaysia	experimental	F
		Thailand	experimental	F
Cirrhina mrigala Mrigal	Cyprinidae	Burma	moderate	F
		Thailand	experimental	F

Sources: Ling, 1972 and 1973; Hora and Pillay, 1962.
A. Comments on many of these species may be found immediately following this table.
B. Environment: F = fresh water; S = salt water or brackish water

TABLE 3. (continued)

PRINCIPAL SPECIES OF FINFISH, SHELLFISH, AND SEAWEEDS BEING CULTURED
OR HAVING HIGH POTENTIAL FOR CULTURING IN SOUTHEAST ASIAN REGION[A]

SCIENTIFIC AND COMMON NAME	FAMILY	COUNTRY WHERE CULTURED	EXTENT OF DEVELOPMENT	ENVIRONMENT[B]
Cirrhina molitorella Bottom carp	Cyprinidae	Hongkong	extensive	F
		Malaysia	moderate	F
		Singapore	moderate	F
		Taiwan	extensive	F
		Thailand	moderate	F
		Vietnam	moderate	F
Catla catla Catla	Cyprinidae	Burma	moderate	F
		Malaysia	experimental	F
		Thailand	experimental	F
Ctenopharyngodon idellus Grass carp	Cyprinidae	All countries	moderate to very extensive	F
Mylopharyngodon piceus Black or snail carp	Cyprinidae	Hongkong	small scale	F
		Taiwan	moderate	F
		Thailand	small scale	F
		Vietnam	small scale	F
Hypophthalmichthys molitrix Silver carp	Cyprinidae	All countries	experimental to very extensive	F
Aristichthys nobilis Bighead carp	Cyprinidae	All countries	experimental to very extensive	F
Osteochilus hasselti Nilem	Cyprinidae	Indonesia	extensive	F
		Malaysia	experimental	F
		Philippines	experimental	F
		Thailand	small scale	F
Clarias batrachus and *Clarias* spp. Walking catfish	Clariidae	Cambodia	small scale	F
		Hongkong	moderate	F
		Malaysia	small scale	F
		Philippines	small scale	F
		Taiwan	moderate	F
		Thailand	extensive	F
		Vietnam	moderate	F

Sources: Ling, 1972 and 1973; Hora and Pillay, 1962.
A. Comments on many of these species may be found immediately following this table.
B. Environment: F = fresh water; S = salt water or brackish water

TABLE 3. (continued)

PRINCIPAL SPECIES OF FINFISH, SHELLFISH, AND SEAWEEDS BEING CULTURED
OR HAVING HIGH POTENTIAL FOR CULTURING IN SOUTHEAST ASIAN REGION[A]

SCIENTIFIC AND COMMON NAME	FAMILY	COUNTRY WHERE CULTURED	EXTENT OF DEVELOPMENT	ENVIRONMENT[B]
Pangasius sutchi and *Pangasius* spp. River catfish	Pangasidae	Cambodia	extensive	F
		Taiwan	experimental	F
		Thailand	extensive	F
		Vietnam	extensive	F
Ophicephalus striatus and *Ophicephalus* spp. Snakehead (Murrel)	Ophicephalidae	Cambodia	extensive	F
		Hongkong	moderate	F
		Laos	moderate	F
		Taiwan	moderate	F
		Thailand	moderate	F
		Vietnam	moderate	F
Helostoma temmincki Kissing gourami	Helostcmidae	Indonesia	extensive	F
		Malaysia	experimental	F
		Thailand	small scale	F
Osphronemus goramy Giant gourami	Osphronemidae	Indonesia	extensive	F
		Malaysia	experimental	F
		Thailand	small scale	F
Trichogaster pectoralis Siamese gourami	Osphronemidae	Indonesia	moderate	F
		Malaysia	extensive	F
		Thailand	extensive	F
Oxyeleotris marmoratus Sand goby	Eleotridae	Hongkong	experimental	F
		Malaysia	experimental	F
		Singapore	experimental	F
		Thailand	experimental	F
		Vietnam	experimental	F

CRUSTACEANS

Penaeus monodon Tiger prawn, grass prawn	Penaeidae	Indonesia	moderate	S
		Malaysia	experimental	S
		Philippines	extensive with milkfish	S
		Singapore	experimental	S
		Taiwan	moderate	S
		Thailand	experimental	S
		Vietnam	experimental	S

Sources: Ling, 1972 and 1973; Hora and Pillay, 1962.
A. Comments on many of these species may be found immediately following this table.
B. Environment: F = fresh water; S = salt water or brackish water

TABLE 3. (continued)

PRINCIPAL SPECIES OF FINFISH, SHELLFISH, AND SEAWEEDS BEING CULTURED OR HAVING HIGH POTENTIAL FOR CULTURING IN SOUTHEAST ASIAN REGION[A]

SCIENTIFIC AND COMMON NAME	FAMILY	COUNTRY WHERE CULTURED	EXTENT OF DEVELOPMENT	ENVIRONMENT[B]
P. japonicus Banded shrimp, Kuruma shrimp	Penaeidae	Indonesia Malaysia Taiwan Thailand Vietnam	experimental experimental moderate experimental experimental	S S S S S
P. merguiensis Bluetail shrimp, Banana shrimp	Penaeidae	Indonesia Malaysia Philippines Singapore Thailand Vietnam	moderate experimental moderate moderate extensive moderate	S S S S S S
P. indicus	Penaeidae	All countries	moderate to extensive	S
P. semisulcatus Red-legged shrimp	Penaeidae	Most countries	experimental	S
Metapenaeus monoceros Sand shrimp	Penaeidae	Most countries	experimental to moderate/extensive	S
M. brevicornis Short-horned shrimp	Penaeidae	Most countries	experimental to moderate	S
Macrobrachium rosenbergii Giant freshwater prawn	Palaemonidae	Cambodia Indonesia Malaysia Philippines Singapore Taiwan Thailand Vietnam	experimental experimental small scale experimental small scale small scale small scale experimental	F F F F F & S F F F
Scylla serrata Mangrove crab	Scyllidae	Hongkong Indonesia Malaysia Philippines Singapore Taiwan Thailand Vietnam	small scale small scale small scale small scale small scale small scale small scale small scale	S S S S S S S S

Sources: Ling, 1972 and 1973; Hora and Pillay, 1962.
A. Comments on many of these species may be found immediately following this table.
B. Environment: F = fresh water; S = salt water or brackish water

TABLE 3. *(continued)*

PRINCIPAL SPECIES OF FINFISH, SHELLFISH, AND SEAWEEDS BEING CULTURED OR HAVING HIGH POTENTIAL FOR CULTURING IN SOUTHEAST ASIAN REGION[A]

SCIENTIFIC AND COMMON NAME	FAMILY	COUNTRY WHERE CULTURED	EXTENT OF DEVELOPMENT	ENVIRONMENT[B]
MOLLUSCS—OYSTERS				
Crassostrea gigas Japanese (Pacific) oyster	Ostreidae	Hongkong Taiwan	extensive extensive	S S
C. malabonensis	Ostreidae	Philippines	extensive	S
C. iredalei	Ostreidae	Philippines Thailand Vietnam	extensive experimental experimental	S S S
C. palmipes	Ostreidae	Philippines	moderate	S
C. cuculata	Ostreidae	Philippines Singapore	moderate experimental	S S
C. lugubris	Ostreidae	Thailand	extensive	S
C. belcheri	Ostreidae	Thailand	extensive	S
C. commercialis	Ostreidae	Thailand	moderate	S
MOLLUSCS—PEARL OYSTERS				
Pinctada martiensii	Pteriidae	Burma Hongkong Indonesia Malaysia Philippines Thailand	moderate moderate moderate moderate moderate moderate	S S S S S S
P. margaritifera	Pteriidae	same as above	moderate	S
P. maxima	Pteriidae	same as above	moderate	S
MOLLUSCS—CLAMS AND MUSSELS				
Meretrix meretrix	Veneridae	Taiwan Vietnam	extensive experimental	S S

Sources: Ling, 1972 and 1973; Hora and Pillay, 1962.
A. Comments on many of these species may be found immediately following this table.
B. Environment: F = fresh water; S = salt water or brackish water

TABLE 3. (continued)

PRINCIPAL SPECIES OF FINFISH, SHELLFISH, AND SEAWEEDS BEING CULTURED[A]
OR HAVING HIGH POTENTIAL FOR CULTURING IN SOUTHEAST ASIA REGION

SCIENTIFIC AND COMMON NAME	FAMILY	COUNTRY WHERE CULTURED	EXTENT OF DEVELOPMENT	ENVIRONMENT[B]
Anadara granosa and *Anadara* spp. Blood clam, cockle	Arcidae	Cambodia	moderate	S
		Indonesia	moderate	S
		Malaysia	extensive	S
		Philippines	moderate	S
		Taiwan	moderate	S
		Thailand	extensive	S
		Vietnam	moderate	S
Mytilus smaragdinus Green sea mussel	Mytidae	Cambodia	moderate	S
		Hongkong	experimental	S
		Indonesia	moderate	S
		Malaysia	moderate	S
		Philippines	extensive	S
		Singapore	experimental	S
		Thailand	extensive	S
		Vietnam	moderate	S
ALGAE				
Porphyra capistrala and *Porphyra* spp. Nori	Bangiaceae	Philippines	experimental	S
		Taiwan	experimental	S
Gracilaria spp.	Gracilariaceae	Indonesia	experimental	S
		Malaysia	experimental	S
		Philippines	experimental	S
		Singapore	experimental	S
		Taiwan	moderate	S
		Thailand	experimental	S
Gelidium sp.	Gelidaceae	Philippines	experimental	S
		Taiwan	experimental	S
Eucheuma spinosum	Solieriaceae	Indonesia	experimental	S
		Philippines	moderate	S
		Singapore	experimental	S
Eucheuma edule	Solieriaceae	Indonesia	experimental	S

Sources: Ling, 1972 and 1973; Hora and Pillay, 1962.
A. Comments on many of these species may be found immediately following this table.
B. Environment: F = fresh water; S = salt water or brackish water

vested and sold before they are one year old. The age of maturity has been estimated to be 5 or 6 years; therefore no mature specimens are found in ponds. There is no oceanic fishery for milkfish; a few mature specimens have been caught in certain localities. No one has yet been able to spawn this fish under controlled conditions; all the fry and fingerlings are collected from the seacoast by hand netting.

ANGUILLA JAPONICA is a freshwater eel. In many Asian countries it is not only considered good-tasting, but is thought to have very high nutritive value and even aphrodisiac properties. This fish spawns in the deep sea; its life history is not yet fully understood, but is probably more or less the same as that of the European eel. It is voraciously carnivorous, feeding on small fish, aquatic worms, and insects. Glass eels are collected for stocking from river mouths during the time they migrate from the sea upstream.

MUGIL CEPHALUS, the grey mullet, is a cosmopolitan species that occurs worldwide. It feeds on plankton and detritus. Its spawning habits are fully understood, and in Taiwan, Hawaii, and Israel the spawning and raising of fry to adulthood have been accomplished successfully. However, the main source of supply of fry and fingerlings is still the natural habitat.

LATES CALCARIFER is the cockup, quite similar to the sea bass in body form and habits. It is a carnivorous, tasty fish with very few bones. Its reproductive habits are still not well known; the source of fish seed is the natural estuarine habitat.

EPINEPHELUS spp. are the groupers. Certain species of groupers are sold as luxury items in Hongkong for over $10 per pound. This fish is still in the early experimental stages of culturing. It is carnivorous, feeding on small fish and crustaceans, but can be fed formulated high protein food. All fish seed is collected from natural waters.

MYLIO MACROCEPHALUS and *CHRYSOPHRYS MAJOR,* the porgy and sea bream, are expensive carnivorous marine fish, feeding on small fish and crustaceans. The young are collected from the sea and cultured in marine water, at present on an experimental basis.

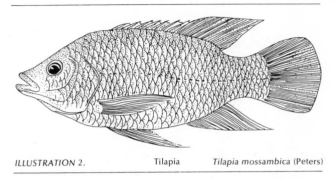

ILLUSTRATION 2.   Tilapia   *Tilapia mossambica* (Peters)

TILAPIA MOSSAMBICA is the source of numerous controversies. When it was first introduced into the Philippines, it was proclaimed as the "wonder fish." Unfortunately, it reproduces so rapidly that a state of overpopulation is soon reached, resulting in a large number of stunted fish and no large individuals. Many people dislike small fish, accounting for its unpopularity. However in Indonesia the people habitually eat tiny fish, and enjoy eating fried *Tilapia* whole. In the Philippines the *Tilapia* interferes with milkfish culture because its nest-building habit destroys the algal mat of the pond, the main source of food for the milkfish.

TILAPIA NILOTICA has been introduced to Asia mainly for the purpose of crossing it with *T. mossambica* to produce fast-growing hybrids that can attain a larger size than either of the parent fish.

PLECOGLOSSUS ALTIVELIS, the sweetfish, or "ayu," is small in size but very high-priced and much prized in Japan, Korea, and Taiwan. It has almost become depleted in Taiwan, where efforts are being made to restock it. This fish is herbivorous, feeding on blue-green

17

algae, diatoms, and small, soft vegetation attached to pebbles and stones in river and stream beds.

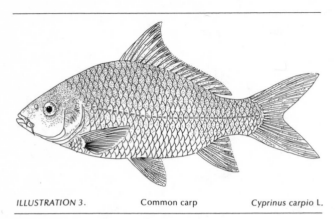

ILLUSTRATION 3.　　　　Common carp　　　　Cyprinus carpio L.

CYPRINUS CARPIO is the common carp. It is omnivorous, and has the habit of browsing at the bottom of the pond, thereby muddying the water. The reproductive habits of this fish are very well known; it is spawned easily almost throughout the year in tropical waters and has been cultured since 1000 B.C. There are several varieties and many subvarieties of the common carp in Southeast Asia, developed to satisfy local preferences. It is the most popular freshwater pond fish in Southeast Asia. Unfortunately, this fish has a bad reputation in the United States.

CARASSIUS AURATUS, the wild goldfish, and CARASSIUS CARASSIUS, the crucian carp, are very similar in body form, food habits, and reproductive habits. Both are plankton and detritus feeders, and can help control mosquito larvae. The former was selectively bred for hundreds of years for beauty, and many ornamental varieties of goldfish have thus been developed, but the original wild type is still popularly eaten. Spawning can be done easily, and fry and fingerlings are being produced extensively in simple hatcheries.

PUNTIUS GONIONOTUS, the Puntius carp, is indigenous to Indonesia, Thailand, Malaysia, and the Philippines. It is herbivorous, grows rapidly, and is cultured in those countries extensively, either alone (monoculture), or in place of grass carp in polyculture systems. This fish is one of the principal species used by the Indonesians in ricefield fish culture. In ponds, this fish can reach sexual maturity within one year and can be easily induced to spawn.

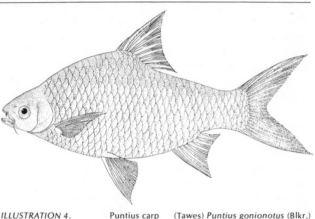

ILLUSTRATION 4.　　　　Puntius carp　　　(Tawes) Puntius gonionotus (Blkr.)

LABEO ROHITA, the rohu, is one of the major carps of the Indian subcontinent that has been introduced to Southeast Asia for culturing. It is a column feeder, consuming zoo and phytoplankton, detritus, and decayed vegetable matter. It is suitable for pond culture; it grows rapidly, is a good food converter, and has good eating quality. In ponds, sexual maturity is reached when the fish is two to three years old, and spawning can be induced by the procedure of hypophyzation.

CIRRHINA MRIGALA, the mrigal, is a freshwater river fish of India and Burma, suitable for culture in ponds in combination with other species. Its fry feed mainly on zooplankton, small crustaceans, and rotifers; adult fish

18

are bottom feeders, subsisting on blue-green and filamentous algae, diatoms, small pieces of higher plants and detritus. It grows rapidly and is highly esteemed as a food fish. In ponds the mrigal reaches sexual maturity in about 2 years. Fry and fingerlings are predominately collected from the natural waters, but increasing quantities are being produced in hatcheries.

CIRRHINA MOLITORELLA, the bottom carp, is one of the major Chinese carps extensively used in polyculture. It does not grow to a large size, but has excellent taste. It feeds primarily on detritus, pieces of plant and animal material accumulated at the pond bottom, and any living minute plants and animals present there. This carp is a subtropical fish and grows best in water with a temperature range of 26-32° C. In ponds it is able to reach sexual maturity in 1-2 years, and can be induced to spawn by using the hormone treatment technique.

CATLA CATLA, the catla, is one of the major carps of India and Burma, famous for its good taste. It is a river fish, suitable for culture in ponds. Fry and fingerlings feed on phytoplankton, zooplankton, diatoms, and microorganisms; young and adults are surface and column feeders, feeding on planktonic organisms, algae, small crustaceans, and decaying plant and animal material. It is an efficient converter and a fast grower; under favorable conditions it is able to grow over 1.5 kg in the first year and over 5 kg by the end of the second year. Formerly, spawning rarely occurred under pond conditions, and all fry were collected from natural waters. At present fry can be produced in hatcheries by the application of hormone treatment to induce spawning.

CTENOPHARYNGODON IDELLUS, the grass carp (white amur), is indeed a wonder fish, ideal for culturing and excellent for control of excessive growth of aquatic vegetation. It is the most efficient macrovegetation-eating fish known and is able to feed on a large variety of aquatic plants as a cow feeds on land grasses. The high efficiency of the grass carp as a macrovegetation feeder

became known to the Western world only after World War II, and since then it has been introduced to many countries on all five continents. However, proposals for its use in the United States, either in pond culture or for stocking in natural waters to control excessive growth of aquatic vegetation, are still the center of controversy. The original home of this fish was China; it occurs mainly in two important river systems—the Yang-tze River (central China) and the West River (south China)

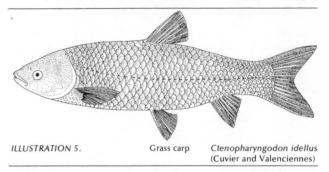

ILLUSTRATION 5.   Grass carp   *Ctenopharyngodon idellus*
                                                 (Cuvier and Valenciennes)

systems—but it is also found in other river systems in north and west China. It is a temperate water fish with a wide range of temperature tolerance and is suitable for culture in tropical as well as temperate waters. It is an excellent converter, grows very rapidly, and has high taste quality. In ponds this fish attains sexual maturity in about 2 years in tropical waters and 3-4 years in temperate waters. Before 1960 all fry were collected from their natural habitats, but at present most of the stocking material is produced in hatcheries by induced spawning.

MYLOPHARYNGODON PICEUS, the black or snail carp, is so named for its dark coloration, especially the fins, and its habit of feeding on snails. It grows more slowly than the grass carp, but is tastier and has a higher market value. It is a bottom feeder, subsisting primarily on snails and clams, and sometimes on worms. This fish is thought to have good potential as a biological control agent for snail populations, especially those that serve as intermediate hosts of dangerous human parasites. Its reproductive habits are similar to those of the grass carp.

HYPOPHTHALMICHTHYS MOLITRIX, the silver carp, so named because of its silvery color, is a plankton feeder, subsisting primarily on phytoplankton, diatoms, and rotifers, and supplementing this diet with soft algae, decaying plant material, and detritus. It is a river fish, able to live in slightly brackish water, and is suitable for culture in ponds. Its efficiency as a phytoplankton feeder makes it a good agent for biological control of phytoplankton blooms in cases of eutrophication due to or-

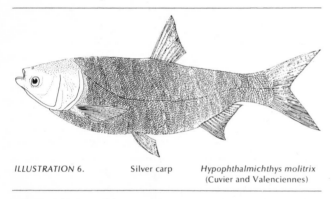

ILLUSTRATION 6.   Silver carp   *Hypophthalmichthys molitrix*
(Cuvier and Valenciennes)

ganic pollution. This fish can tolerate a wide range of water temperatures, is easy to cultivate, grows rapidly, and can become sexually mature when 1-2 years old in tropical water and 2-3 years old in temperate waters. In ponds this fish does not spawn naturally unless given hormone treatment. At present most fry and fingerlings are produced in hatcheries by the induced spawning method.

ARISTICHTHYS NOBILIS, the bighead carp, is quite similar to the silver carp in general body form and reproductive habits. It is an efficient plankton feeder, feeding primarily on zooplankton, but is also able to make use of decaying organic substances and detritus. It is a fast grower, and is well known for its large head, which is

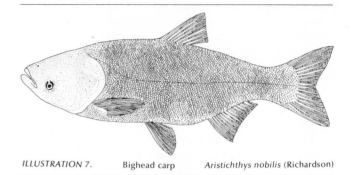

ILLUSTRATION 7.   Bighead carp   *Aristichthys nobilis* (Richardson)

highly esteemed by the Chinese. By weight, the price of the head of this fish is usually as high as, or sometimes even higher than, that of its body. Formerly all fry were collected from natural waters; at present most are produced in hatcheries by the induced spawning technique.

OSTEOCHILUS HASSELTI, known as Nilem in Indonesia, is a river and lake fish suitable for pond culture. It is a tropical water fish and unable to tolerate cold water temperatures. It feeds on microorganisms, soft algae, diatoms, protozoans, and decayed plant substances by nibbling, rasping, or sucking. In ponds it can attain sexual maturity at the end of the first year when about 15-20 cm in length, and can be induced to spawn by a strong flow of running water. For large-scale production of fry, special spawning ponds with beds of coarse gravel, pebbles, or small stones, and provisions for a strong flow of clean, fresh, running water, are constructed.

CLARIAS BATRACHUS, the common catfish of Asia, sometimes erroneously called the "walking catfish," is a Labyrinthici, possessing well-developed accessory respiratory organs in its head. It has a scaleless, elongated body, a depressed head, and four pairs of barbels on its mouth. It occurs in many kinds of stagnant water, in ricefields, swamps, marshes, ponds, and water canals. Fry feed on microorganisms; adults feed on small fish, crustaceans, insect larvae, and organic detritus. This cat-

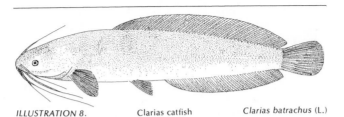

ILLUSTRATION 8.   Clarias catfish   Clarias batrachus (L.)

fish is able to tolerate water highly polluted with organic matter and containing little oxygen, and is suitable for high density cultivation. Sexual maturity is reached when the fish is about 1 year old, and spawning can take place in ponds as well as in its natural habitat. It is a tasty fish, well liked by people of Southeast Asia.

PANGASIUS SUTCHI, a river catfish of Thailand and the Indochina region, is suitable for cultivation in ponds and floating cages. It is both fast-growing and tasty, and occurs in lakes, water reservoirs, rivers, and irrigation canals. It is primarily omnivorous, occasionally feeding on small fish and other small animals. In ponds, the fish is fed various kinds of kitchen waste, spoiled fish, spoiled fruits, and a mixture of cooked rice, trash fish, rice bran, and soft aquatic plants. It is the principal species of fish cultured in the famous floating cages of Cambodia and Thailand.

   Fry and fingerlings are primarily collected from natural habitats; some are produced in the hatchery by induced spawning. Fish are usually harvested from ponds or cages after 10-12 months of cultivation, when they weight about 1.5 kg each. Fish caught in open waters weight about 3-5 kg each; fish weighing over 10 kg are commonly caught.

OPHIOCEPHALUS STRIATUS, the snakehead fish or murrel, is a freshwater fish with a well-developed accessory respiratory organ. It is able to tolerate water with low oxygen content and is even able to survive for quite a while out of water in a moist environment. It is meaty and tasty, and highly esteemed as a food fish. The snakehead occurs in swamps, lakes, water reservoirs,

farm ponds, and ricefields. It is highly carnivorous, feeding on small fish, crustaceans, insects, and worms. It is cultured in floating cages or in ponds, and fed heavily. Maturity is reached at one year of age, and spawning can take place in confined waters as well as natural environments.

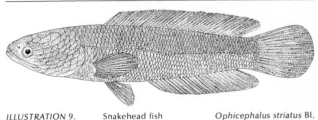

ILLUSTRATION 9.   Snakehead fish   Ophicephalus striatus Bl.

HELOSTOMA TEMMINCKI, the kissing gourami, are so-called for the habit of occasionally sucking each others' mouths. This is a freshwater fish, with an oblong-oval body and a very protractile mouth with thick lips. It occurs in swamps, shallow lakes, water reservoirs, and rivers and is suitable for culture in tropical ponds. This fish is a very efficient plankton feeder and is able to make use of most kinds of phytoplankton and diatoms. It possesses an accessory respiratory organ and is a good fish for stocking in waters polluted by organic matter and suffering from phytoplankton blooms. Sexual maturity is attained when the fish is 1 year old; spawning can be induced in small ponds, cement tanks, or aquariums by the provision of clean, fresh water.

OSPHRONEMUS GORAMY, the giant gourami, is known for its large size among the gourami group. The body is strongly compressed; the mouth is small with protractile lips. It occurs in rivers, lakes, water reservoirs, and swamps; and it is suitable for culture in tropical ponds. The fry feed on microorganisms; fingerlings feed on small crustaceans, insects, and worms; young and adult feed mainly on the tender parts of aquatic plants and on algae. The fish is a slow grower, but it is very tasty and is

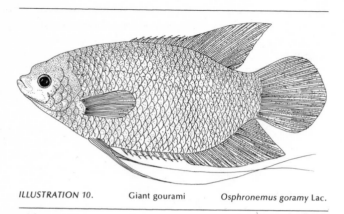

ILLUSTRATION 10.   Giant gourami   *Osphronemus goramy* Lac.

highly esteemed by the Indonesians. It attains sexual maturity in about 3 years, builds a nest, and lays eggs inside it. In ponds the fish may be fed leaves and tender parts of *Ipomoea*, several kinds of land grass, banana, yam, tapioca, kitchen waste, or a mixture of cooked rice, rice bran, and trash fish.

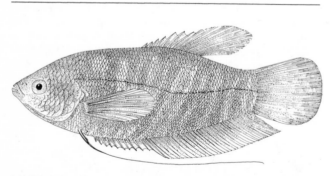

ILLUSTRATION 11.   Siamese gourami   *Trichogaster pectoralis* Regan

TRICHOGASTER PECTORALIS, the Siamese gourami or Sepat Siam, lives in swamps, water canals, ricefields, water reservoirs, lakes, and rivers, and is suitable for culture in ponds or ricefields. It feeds on many kinds of phyto- and zooplankton, diatoms, small crustaceans, worms, decaying organic substances, and detritus. It is a

small fish; average market size is about 130 grams, which is attained after about 8 months of cultivation. This fish is not very tasty in its fresh state, but it is highly esteemed when processed as dried fish. Sexual maturity is reached after 6-7 months; spawning takes place during the rainy season in either open waters or ponds.

OXYELEOTRIS MARMORATUS, the sand goby, has a cylindrical, slightly elongated body, and a blunt head with a large mouth. It occurs in lakes, mining pools, water reservoirs, and swamps. It is carnivorous, feeding primarily on small fish, crustaceans, insects, and worms, but can be trained to take protein-rich supplemental feeds. This fish grows rapidly when well fed and is able to attain a weight of 900 grams in one year. Its flesh has a fine texture and high taste quality, and it is regarded as a luxury item. Sexual maturity is reached after one year, and spawning can be induced under controlled conditions. The supply of fry and fingerlings still comes primarily from natural habitats.

PENAEUS MONODON, jumbo tiger prawn (known as "grass prawn" in Taiwan). This is one of the largest penaeids; females weighing over 250 grams have been recorded. Average market size of these shrimps is usually 150 grams for the female. and 90 grams for the male. *P. monodon* occurs abundantly in Southeast Asian waters, usually offshore in depths of about 20-25 fathoms. The shell of the shrimp is smooth and polished, with a few blue spots scattered on a pale brown background. Broad, transverse bands of light and dark shades alternate along the dorsal half of the body. *P. monodon* is hardy, able to tolerate a wide range of salinities and water temperatures. Fast growing, it feeds on matter of both plant and animal origin. It has long been popularly cultured in Southeast Asian brackish-water ponds, especially in the Philippines and Taiwan, and is regarded as one of the best species with high potential for commercial farming development. Before 1970 all *P. monodon* postlarvae used for pond culture were collected from their natural habitats of tidal canals, mangrove swamps, and other brackish-water areas. Since then, postlarvae have been successfully produced in hatcheries in Taiwan, the Philippines, and Indonesia, and the number of postlarvae from this source has increased steadily to help meet growing demands from rapidly expanding prawn farming operations.

PENAEUS JAPONICUS, banded shrimp or Kuruma shrimp. This is the best known cultivable penaeid shrimp. Pioneering research on the life history and larval rearing of penaeid shrimp was performed successfully on this species in Japan, initiating the development of modern shrimp culture. Many spawning, hatching, and farming techniques for this species developed in Japan are now being used worldwide as a basis for the study and development of commercial shrimp farming of many other species of penaeid. *P. japonicus* is a large shrimp; female specimens weighing over 150 grams are commonly caught. It is distributed widely, from Japan, Korea, and China, through the countries bordering the South China Sea, to the east coast of India. It prefers sandy bottoms in coastal waters less than 150 meters deep. The shrimp buries itself during the day and is active at night. It grows rapidly, feeding primarily on food of animal origin, but has poor tolerance of low oxygen and salinity levels, or high water temperatures.

The body of *P. japonicus* is beautifully colored. It is a light brown or greenish grey striped with ten to eleven broad, transverse bands of deep brown. Its tail fan is colored deep brown, light yellow, light brown, yellow, and blue in succession from margin to base. The walking legs and swimmerets are yellow, pale green, and pink. This shrimp is the most expensive one in Japan; live specimens often cost more than $10 per pound in the Tokyo market.

PENAEUS MERGUIENSIS, bluetail shrimp (or banana shrimp). A medium-large shrimp, well liked by the people for its delicate texture and taste. It occurs abundantly in coastal and estuarine waters throughout the year. The body surface of the shrimp is smooth and predominantly light brownish yellow in color (banana-colored). The tail fans are blue; hence it is known as "bluetail" shrimp in Thailand. *P. merguiensis* is one of the most important penaeids that has commonly been harvested in the traditional type of shrimp ponds in Southeast Asia. The postlarvae and juveniles enter brackish-water ponds in large numbers where they thrive, growing rapidly. This shrimp can tolerate wide ranges of salinity and temperature. It is fast becoming an important shrimp in commercial farming ventures. Moderate production of postlarvae in hatcheries for stocking has already been successfully achieved.

PENAEUS INDICUS is a species closely related to *P. merguiensis,* having very similar biology and habits. It is slightly smaller and can tolerate very dilute saline waters. This species has great potential for commercial shrimp farming.

PENAEUS SEMISULCATUS, red-legged shrimp. This species is smaller than *P. monodon,* but is very similar in body form. It is slightly lighter in color with fainter transverse bands, and its walking legs and swimmerets are red, giving it the common name of red-legged shrimp. The life cycle of *P. semisulcatus* is also quite similar to that of *P. monodon,* and postlarvae and juveniles are often found in estuarine areas. However, young shrimp tend to migrate seaward; they prefer sandy bottoms and cannot tolerate low salinity or high temperatures. *P. semisulcatus* feeds primarily on food of animal origin. It does not survive well in the existing, traditional type of shallow mud ponds in Southeast Asia.

METAPENAEUS MONOCEROS, sand shrimp. A medium-sized shrimp, very popular throughout Asia not only as food but as fish bait. The shell is thick, and its whole surface is covered with numerous irregular narrow grooves and minute setae. The body is pale grey or pale olive with many faint dark spots. *M. monoceros* occurs abundantly year-round in shallow coastal waters, estuaries, and mangrove swamps. It prefers sandy bottoms and often lies half-buried in the sand during the day. It can thrive in waters with salinity as low as 10°/oo. The sand shrimp feeds on material of both plant and animal origin and grows rapidly. It is often cultured in traditional shrimp ponds, especially with milkfish. M. monoceros is easily cultured in high densities in brackish-water ponds with a high survival rate. It can grow to market size in 2 months. In spite of its moderate size, this shrimp has great potential for large-scale commercial farming.

METAPENAEUS BREVICORNIS, short-horned shrimp. A medium-sized shrimp with a smooth shell and very short rostrum. It thrives in waters with salinity as low as 3-4°/oo, and grows rapidly on food of plant and animal origin. This shrimp has good potential for commercial farming.

MACROBRACHIUM ROSENBERGII, giant freshwater prawn. This is the largest prawn in Asia. Male specimens weighing over 200 grams are often caught, and specimens weighing over 500 grams have been recorded. It is widely distributed in Southeast Asia, India, Ceylon, and Bangladesh, and since time immemorial has been highly esteemed as food. M. rosenbergii has a large cephalothorax. The second pair of walking legs is extremely long, especially in males, often reaching one and one-half times the body length. The shell is olive green to greyish in color. M. rosenbergii occurs year-round in both fresh and brackish waters. It inhabits most of the rivers in Southeast Asia, especially the lower reaches, which are influenced by tides, although it also occurs over 200 kilometers upstream from river mouths and is present in lakes, water reservoirs, mining pools, canals, and even some paddyfields which have access to rivers. The prawn may spend the period of its life cycle from juvenile to adult entirely in fresh water, but its larval stages can survive only in saline water. The larval stages are planktonic, feeding on zooplankton and possibly other particles of animal origin. Juveniles and adults feed primarily on material of animal origin although they are able to utilize plant material. M. rosenbergii grows rapidly, converts food efficiently, and is extremely suitable for prawn farming.

SCYLLA SERRATA, mangrove crab. The mangrove crab is the most important crab in the Southeast Asian region. It occurs year-round, but most abundantly during October to March, in shallow estuarine waters, mangrove swamps, tidal flats, tidal canals, and brackish-water pools and ponds, where it prefers muddy bottoms and areas rich in organic material. During low tide the mangrove crab hides in holes to avoid exposure to strong sunlight and enemies. It feeds actively, on animal food, at night or when light is dim. The carapace of S. serrata is fanlike, and its surface is smooth and grayish-green in color. The chelipeds are strong and robust. The mangrove crab grows rapidly and attains sexual maturity when about 1 year old. Mating and spawning usually take place in clear coastal waters. Larvae are planktonic and feed on zooplankton. Experiments on rearing larval stages to juveniles under controlled conditions have been conducted in Malaysia, the Philippines, and Thailand with varying degrees of success. Practical techniques for commercial production of juveniles in hatcheries have not yet been developed. Young crabs used for stocking are presently collected from natural habitats. Chopped trash fish is the principal feed used in their culture. A highly profitable practice is the fattening of "green crabs" (females with immature ovaries). These female crabs can be obtained very cheaply, and are heavily fed on trash fish to promote rapid development of the ovaries. Female mangrove crabs with full ovaries are highly esteemed as food and command a much higher market price than males. Common market size of mangrove crabs ranges from 12-16 centimeters in carapace width.

CRASSOSTREA GIGAS, Japanese oyster. Among the handful of oyster species cultured in Southeast Asia, the Japanese oyster, C. gigas, is the most important, and has great potential for commercial farming. Presently Taiwan has the greatest acreage of oyster farms, followed by the Philippines and Hongkong, Thailand, and Vietnam. The abundant natural supply of food and nutrients, year-round high water temperatures, and extensive estuarine and coastal areas found there favor rapid growth of oysters. However, such seemingly favorable factors can also become liabilities. Constant high water temperature induces continuous spawning of oysters, resulting in overcrowded oyster beds and flesh of poor market quality. Culturing methods are predominantly simple and traditional; modern farming techniques are still at an early stage of development. In many oyster-farming areas in this region, there is not much separation between spat-collecting grounds and oyster-growing and fattening grounds. The popularly practiced method used in Taiwan for both spat-collection and oyster-growing is the planting of bamboo sticks or poles in the shallow bottoms of suitable tidal flats. This method, requiring little investment, is cheap, simple, easily manageable, and highly productive, but it is labor-intensive.

ANADARA GRANOSA, blood clam, cockle. This rib-shelled bivalve has red blood, hence its common name. It occurs in many estuarine and intertidal mud flats, and can thrive in waters with a seasonal salinity fluctuation of 18-30°/oo. It grows rapidly, becoming sexually mature at about 1 year of age. The peak spawning period is between June and October. Larvae of this cockle are planktonic; the location, density, and timing of spatfall vary from year to year. The cockle is extensively cultured in most Southeast Asian countries, especially Malaysia, Thailand, Indonesia, Vietnam, and Taiwan. It is very popular in this region. Seed cockles are collected from natural beds when they are about 4 months old, measuring from 4-10 mm in size. They are quickly transported to culture beds and sown there immediately. The cockles grow to acceptable (legal) market size (31-35 mm) about 8-9 months after sowing. Harvesting is carried out over a period of 2-3 months.

MYTILUS SMARAGDINUS (M. viridis), green sea mussel. This fairly large, green sea mussel, with pronounced green along the outer margin of the shell, occurs abundantly in Southeast Asian waters where it is a popular, inexpensive protein food. It grows rapidly in estuaries and coastal waters rich in plankton and/or organic matter and can thrive in salinities ranging from 20-30°/oo and temperatures ranging from 20-28°C. *M. smaragdinus* is hardy, easy to culture, and extremely productive, being one of the most efficient converters of phytoplankton into animal flesh. It has been recognized as one of the most valuable aquatic organisms, with greatest potential for extensive mass aquaculture production, as a high-quality, cheap animal protein food for the people. The sexes of the green sea mussel are separate; maturity is reached when the organism is about 1 year old. Spawning takes place during the winter part of the year, but peak periods usually coincide with monsoon seasons. Mussel larvae are planktonic for about 3 weeks, then settle on some substrate where they undergo a primary and secondary settlement stage before permanently attaching to a suitable substrate to complete their growth.

ALGAE Various species of seaweeds have been used by people of this region for centuries as food and for medicinal and industrial purposes. Supplies have come from local natural resources or through importation. Farming of seaweeds is of recent introduction, and is still in the early stages of development. The principal kinds of seaweed cultured are *Eucheuma* spp., *Gracilaria* spp., and *Porphyra* spp.

EUCHEUMA is a red alga, growing naturally on rocks, reefs, and even sandy bottoms of intertidal and subtidal zones. It thrives in tropical and subtropical regions where the water is clear and swift-moving, with a salinity over 30°/oo. This alga is used for food as well as for the extraction of carrageenan.

GRACILARIA is also a red alga, used primarily for the extraction of agar, although it has also been used as food. Culture of *Gracilaria* is being performed fairly successfully in Taiwan in shallow coastal flats and ponds. This culture has a short history of only 15 years, but is expanding steadily.

PORPHYRA is the famous "nori" (laver) highly esteemed as food by the Japanese, Koreans, and Chinese. Culture techniques developed in Japan have been introduced for experimentation in the Philippines with encouraging results. Significant problems in development of algal culture in Southeast Asia are: (1) climatic limitations; (2) increasing pollution of coastal waters; (3) lack of seaweed farming tradition, technical know-how, and experienced personnel.

4 Collection and Production of Stocking Material

Stocking material, also known as seed, collectively includes fry, larvae, fingerlings, or juveniles of the organism to be cultured. To know where and how to get the seed, it is first necessary to know something about the organism's reproductive habits, both in the wild and under culture conditions. In their natural habitats most organisms proceed through a characteristic life cycle that includes development of the embryo to hatching; growth of the larvae to fry, fingerling and juvenile stages; maturation to the adult stage, accompanied by development of gonads and ripening of ova and spermatozoa; mating, spawning, and fertilization of eggs; and so on through a second generation.

Succeeding events in the reproductive cycle are brought about by the conjunction of internal and external factors. Among the internal factors, the pituitary gland (hypophysis) is considered most crucial; it secretes inhibitory and promoting substances that regulate sexual development and reproductive activities. Important external factors include water conditions (e.g. temperature, flow rate, turbidity, oxygen content, pH), light intensity, length of day, and meteorological conditions such as rain, monsoons, floods, or drought. These external factors act as necessary stimuli to bring about sexual development and spawning activity by somehow affecting the secretion of various hormones. When fish are transplanted to culturing facilities, they are subjected to a new environment, which may upset normal gonadal development or reproductive activity. Under cultural conditions, some fish fail to become sexually mature; others attain sexual maturity but cannot spawn or ovulate. Carp have been known to burst in ponds from overdeveloped gonads.

Details of the reproductive physiology, spawning requirements, and spawning habits of many of the cultured species in Southeast Asia are still not fully understood. Yet sources of fry and fingerlings are well known, and efficient techniques for their collection and han-dling are widely practiced. In some cases, methods of spawning the fish under controlled conditions have been developed for practical use.

There are two main sources of fish seed: the natural environment, or production under controlled conditions in hatcheries.

Stocking Material Collected From Natural Sources

Most fish seed used for stocking and culturing is still collected from natural habitats for economic reasons. Not only is it usually cheaper to collect fry than to produce them in hatcheries, but fry collecting is a well-established industry in most Southeast Asian countries, providing many employment opportunities. Fish seed that can be obtained only from the wild (e.g. milkfish, freshwater eel, and grouper seed) are sought as well as large quantities of fry of those fish that can be spawned (e.g. Chinese major carps, grey mullet, catfish, snakehead).

Collecting areas are found, in order of importance, in freshwater, brackish, and marine environments. From rivers we obtain carps and other groups of fish that require large amounts of oxygen. From swamps, ricefields, and reservoirs, characterized by more stagnant water, we obtain catfish, snakehead, and Siamese gourami, whose accessory breathing organs enable them to survive in water of low oxygen content. Brackish-water areas, characterized by coastal tidelands, are the source primarily of milkfish, grey mullet, and freshwater eel fry. The grey mullet and milkfish are marine fish that spawn in the sea. Their larvae are carried by currents and tides into the coastal estuarine areas. The freshwater eels spawn in deep sea waters. Their planktonic larvae spend several months slowly developing while drifting to coastal areas. They are usually intercepted at the entrance to rivers when they begin to travel upstream. The coastal marine areas are a source of sea bream, grouper, and porgy fry.

I would like to describe to you the centuries-old method used by the Chinese to collect their major carp fry. Not only is it fascinating, but it contains much food for thought. Until about 1960 none of the Chinese major carps had been successfully spawned in waters outside their natural spawning grounds. All fry and fingerlings were collected near those spawning grounds, which were usually quite distant from the culturing centers, sometimes over 200-300 miles away. Location of the fry and subsequent collection, sorting, care, and long-distance transportation required considerable expertise. Every spring fish farmers waited until they heard the first rumblings of thunder—Heaven's signal. They promptly prepared their fry-collecting gear, boats, and provisions and began their journey upstream. It would sometimes take a week or more to travel from their homes to good prospective collecting grounds in the uninhabited wilderness along the Yang-tze River in Central China or the Pearl River in South China, or some other fry-producing river. When they arrived at their destination, the collectors set up camp, establishing a boom town for the duration of the fry-collecting period, complete with temporary stores. Old masters would go into the river, study the water, scoop up a few pails, and carefully examine their contents. As soon as they saw anything resembling fish eggs or spawn, they set up long conical collecting nets and sent scouts upstream to check for young hatchlings. The fry were usually on their way.

The thunder, you see, had signalled the beginning of the rainy season upstream. Heavy rain had flooded the upland and poured into the rivers, increasing the water velocity and raising both the water level and water temperature. These factors had stimulated the parent fish to congregate at the spawning grounds, engage in spawning play, and complete mass spawning. The fertilized eggs, tiny little dots when spawned, had swollen to over 50 times their original volume within one-half hour of contact with the water. Balloonlike,

they floated with the water current from the spawning ground to the collecting ground, usually within 2 days. During this time the embryos had developed and hatched. Now the young hatchlings were caught in the conical nets set at strategic locations along the river and put into special waterproof baskets.

It was the job of the old masters not only to know where and how to collect, but after collecting, to remove undesirable fish and separate the larval carps by species. As we know, it is difficult to identify fish larvae; to distinguish larval fish of related genera often involves the time-consuming process of counting somites and other body characters. Yet the old masters were required to separate millions of these tiny young hatchlings in the field within a few hours and without the aid of microscopes. And they could do it. One of the methods popularly practiced was as follows: The master first put all the larval fish into a huge waterproof bamboo basket filled with fresh river water. While most of the fry of culturable species swam in one direction close to the basket edge, those of undesirable fish (consisting mostly of predatory species not suitable for culture) swam zig-zag, back and forth with no discipline; these were scooped out and thrown away. After removing these "wild" fish, the master took a cup of water and sprinkled it onto the water in the basket, tapped the basket a bit, and then waited quietly. At first the fry swam about excitedly, but they soon stratified into layers in the water column. The top layer of fish was quickly skimmed off into another container. The master tapped the basket again; if more larvae came to the surface, they were added to the first batch. The next layer of fish was then removed, and this was repeated until all the fish had segregated.

Chinese fish fry masters have been practicing this technique for over a thousand years, yet it was not until as recently as 50 years ago that fisheries biologists discovered the scientific reasons behind this natural stratification. The first layer of fish (or those that come up to the top layer of water first) is composed predominantly of silver carp because silver carp fry require the most oxygen. Bighead carp make up the bulk of the second layer, grass carp aggregate in the middle (coming up to the surface of the water later), and the mud carp, requiring the least amount of oxygen, remain below (coming to the surface last). This is just one example of how we are only beginning to understand many of the useful traditional practices begun centuries ago. It would be interesting to see if the fry of American temperate fish also stratify, or whether oriental fish are more disciplined.

Stocking Material Produced Under Controlled Conditions

This category includes all those fry produced under controlled conditions in hatcheries or nurseries. Methods of varying complexity are involved.

NATURAL SPAWNING. The simplest method of fish breeding requires only a fish pond as a facility and is exemplified by the propagation of *Tilapia mossambica*. This fish adapts to a number of pond conditions, grows rapidly, matures quickly, and reproduces readily. Eggs are incubated in the mother's mouth until they hatch. The male tilapia first selects a suitable area in the pond and scoops out a shallow, saucer-shaped depression, 1-2 feet in diameter and 3-4 inches in depth. He then courts a female and brings her to inspect the nest. If she is satisfied, they perform a nuptial dance and embrace just above the pit. The female discharges her eggs as the male discharges milt simultaneously, fertilizing the eggs as they descend. Before the fertilized eggs can drop to the bottom, the female quickly dives down and picks them up one by one in her mouth. This process is repeated several times until the female has spawned all her eggs. An average-sized female tilapia can lay 150-200 eggs. The eggs hatch in the oral cavity within 3 to 5 days and are kept in the mouth for another 4-5 days until the fry can swim actively. Then, if no danger is imminent, the mother opens her mouth and lets the young fry swim out beside her. At the first sign of danger, she opens her mouth and quickly collects the fry. The tilapia becomes sexually mature at the age of 3 months and is then able to spawn every 2-3 months. Overpopulation and subsequent stunting problems are common with this fish.

This brings us to a fundamental principle of fish reproduction. Those fish that exert parental care for their youngsters produce only a small number of eggs. Because the eggs are well protected, a high percentage will survive through the developmental stages to become fingerlings. On the other hand, those fish that do not provide parental protection lay large numbers of eggs to counteract the numerous unknown hazards their young will be exposed to. Some of the Chinese carp produce nearly a million eggs, the grey mullet even more, and a large mature milkfish is capable of producing 2-3 million eggs.

INDUCED SPAWNING. Some fish will spawn under controlled conditions only if properly induced. Several basic steps are taken in all methods of induced spawning. First, fully sexually mature fish with desired characteristics are selected from the brood stock; they are then sexed and kept segregated for 1 to 2 days. When a spawning pond has been drained, cleaned, and refilled, and any additional preparations have been completed, the previously selected and segregated brood stock is introduced. Fish that can be induced to spawn without further preparation include the *Puntius* carp (an Indonesian carp), the nilem, and the kissing gourami.

Sexing fish is itself a task. Many fish must be examined closely, using the proper method. First the belly of the fish is stroked slowly and gently; with one hand at the head and the other around the back (as one would hold a baby), one quickly turns it upside down. The fish usually quiets down, possibly because of a loss of balance or direction. This trick is applicable to many kinds of fish, especially those cultured in Southeast Asia. Once the fish is upside down, it can be examined. Often the

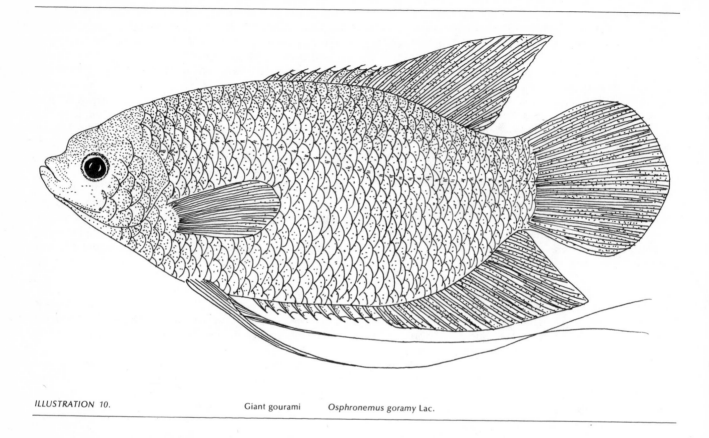

ILLUSTRATION 10.　　　　　　Giant gourami　　*Osphronemus goramy* Lac.

fish will have secondary sexual characters when mature. The male giant gourami develops a large hump over the forehead; the male Siamese gourami has the hind tip of its dorsal fin overreaching its peduncle (while the female does not). The Chinese, Indian, and Indonesian major carps exhibit the following sexual characteristics when mature. Small tubercles develop on the upper surface and edges of the pectoral fins that feel rough to the touch. Male carps are usually much rougher than females on both the fins and cheeks. Beginners often as-sume that big-bellied fish are female, but a male fish may boast a large belly immediately after a heavy meal. One of the simplest ways to sex a mature fish is to press its belly slightly. If the fish is a female and is ripe, eggs will be extruded; mature males yield a small drop of milt. To insure that eggs are in the proper stage of ripe-ness for induced spawning or artificial fertilization, a small catheterlike tube may be inserted through the cloaca into the hind part of the ovary and several eggs extracted and examined under a microscope.

NEST BUILDERS: The simplest type of nest breeder requires only a clear space or area in which to build its nest; a good example is the snakehead. Snakehead spawning ponds are provided with tufts of aquatic plants placed along the water edge and small floating branches scattered on the water surface. The snakehead typically finds a secluded area and then clears it of debris; a precleared area will not be used. After removing the branches provided, the male fish forms a clear space about 1 foot in diameter among the weeds, and then selects a female. The male and female snakeheads spawn beneath the cleared area, and the fertilized eggs, each carrying some large oil globules, float to the surface. The parent fish remain below the nest, guarding the eggs until they hatch and the young fry are able to feed on small protozoans and crustaceans. For an additional 2-3 weeks, the male follows the brood of fry around, providing parental protection. During this time the fingerlings go through an air-breathing development stage; they come to the surface for air then dive back down, at first singly, then all together, while the father remains below.

Bubble nest builders such as the Siamese gourami are provided with cleared areas among aquatic weeds in which to build their nests.

The Siamese gourami will seldom spawn in a pond without weeds to protect its fragile bubble nest. After cleaning the intended spawning pond and replenishing it with fresh water, the fish farmer places aquatic plants in strategic areas. After selecting a well-protected spot, the male Siamese gourami blows bubbles to the water surface to form a nest about 4-5 inches in diameter. He then selects a female and brings her to the nest. After a brief spawning play, mating occurs just beneath the nest with simultaneous discharge of sexual elements. Both fish then quickly dive down, pick up the fertilized eggs, and blow them into the bubble nest. The small eggs require much oxygen for their rapid development and could not develop on the bottom of the pond. The bubble nest helps to keep them afloat as well as provide protection. A small oil globule at one end of the egg

also aids in keeping them afloat. The parent fish remain underneath the nest, driving away enemies and aerating the surrounding water with their swimming currents. When the eggs have hatched and the fry can feed themselves (approximately 4-5 days later), the parent fish leave them. Siamese fighting fish have similar breeding habits.

The giant gourami constructs an elaborate nest like that of a large bird. The exterior of the nest is rough, but the inside chamber is lined with very soft material such as long plant fibers, roots and stems of tender aquatic plants, or even human hair. The fish farmer usually provides the fish with a nest frame and nest fibers. The frame is made of a section of bamboo rod about 2 feet in length. One end is split and the strips are spread into a funnel shape and bound with rings. The other end

FIGURE 2.

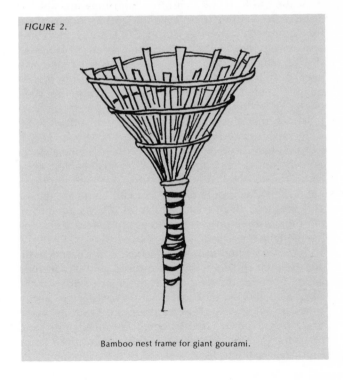

Bamboo nest frame for giant gourami.

31

(the stalk) is bound tight. These frames are inserted into the pond bank by the stalk end where they are shaded and protected by trees and shrubs. Fibers may be placed inside the funnel for the fish to utilize as lining material. The male and female discharge their sexual elements into the inside chamber of the nest through an opening which they later plug with additional fibers. Fertilization of eggs occurs within the nest. The eggs of the giant gourami require a great deal of oxygen. Since this kind of nest restricts water flow, the parent fish constantly swim nearby, fanning their pectoral fins vigorously to propel oxygenating water currents through the nest.

The eggs hatch inside the nest within 3-4 days. Giant gourami hatchlings, resembling tadpoles in shape, cannot swim and so remain in the nest up to 10 days until their yolk is fully absorbed and they are able to swim actively. They then leave the nest as independent fry. During the spawning season, fish farmers search the spawning ponds every day for gourami nests. Although the fish may build their nests in the spots where the artificial nest frames and fibers have been planted, frequently they move them to locations more to their liking. When the nest has been found, the fish farmer must determine if eggs have already been laid within it. If the nest is disturbed before the eggs have been laid, it will be abandoned by the parent fish. The presence of an oily substance above the nest accompanied by a characteristic smell is a reliable sign that eggs are present. When giant gourami eggs are laid, some are invariably crushed; since each egg carries a large amount of oil, the crushing of just 4 or 5 eggs produces visible oil patches above the nest.

The egg-filled nest is detached into a large basin and brought to shore. There slow and gentle loosening of the fibers of the nest causes the eggs to float to the surface of the basin. They are then transferred with a spoon to another shallow earthenware basin in which they are taken to the hatchery for incubation and hatching. In the hatchery, a steady supply of fresh, cool, well-oxygenated water is slowly directed over them.

Fish such as the walking catfish (*Clarias*) dig long tunnels in the embankments of a pond in which they lay their eggs. In the case of the *Clarias* catfish, the tunnels are about 4-5 inches in diameter and 1 foot long. The slightly adhesive eggs cling to the sides of the tunnel. Parent fish remain inside guarding the eggs until they hatch and the young leave as independent fry. Fish farmers provide such fish with artificial tunnels made of clay, cement, or even plastic pipe of the approximate size and shape of normal nests. Special banks may be constructed with holes in them.

ADHESIVE EGG-LAYERS: Some fish, such as the common carp and goldfish, require material on which to attach their adhesive eggs. In the case of the common carp, special preparation is necessary to assure successful spawning and attachment of eggs. In Europe the small Dubish spawning pond, about 100-500 sq ft in surface area, is commonly used. In such a pond prior to the spawning season, land grasses are grown within the dried pond until they reach about 2 feet in height. When the parent fish have been selected and properly conditioned, the Dubish pond is filled with clean, well-oxygenated water and the parent fish are released there. Spawning usually takes place after midnight and by the next morning numerous eggs will be attached to the grasses.

In Southeast Asia, other simple methods have been developed using various materials as egg catchers. Aquatic plants with fine leaves, stems, or root systems (e.g. *Ceretophyllum*, *Hydrilla* (*Elodea*), *Chara*, *Eichornia*) have been found suitable. These plants are collected and bundled. The bundles are tied at intervals along a rope. Four to five ropes of these aquatic plants may be stretched across a pond in parallel rows and tied to poles at each end. When the parent fish are first released into the pond, usually late in the afternoon, they are timid and quiet. After a few hours they begin playing and courting each other, at first gently, but progressively more vigorously. By midnight they have become highly excited and are jumping and splashing over the rows of

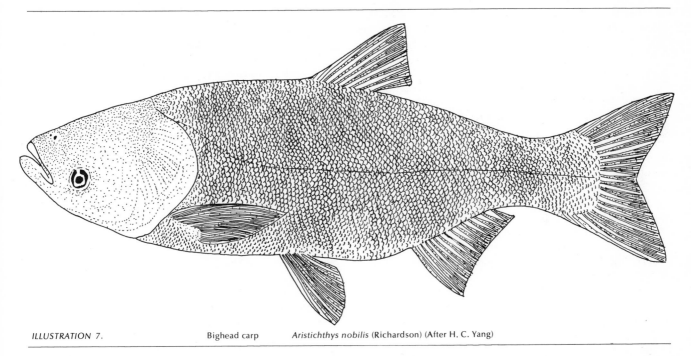

ILLUSTRATION 7.   Bighead carp   *Aristichthys nobilis* (Richardson) (After H. C. Yang)

plants, releasing eggs and milt as they do so. By morning fertilized eggs are found attached to the aquatic weeds. The eggs may be left in the spawning pond or transferred to another prepared pond for incubation and hatching. Palm fibers, Spanish moss, and synthetic fibers (waste material from synthetic factories) are also employed in place of aquatic plants. The fibers are laid crossways between two bamboo rods that are then lashed together. These units are laid one by one across the pond a few inches beneath the water surface. Fish will spawn over these units, and fertilized eggs will attach to the fibers. Synthetic fibers are preferable to living plants in that they can be prepared in advance; they can be cleaned, dried, and reused; they are easy to obtain in a variety of sizes; and being inert, they do not compete with the eggs for oxygen and are not subject to decay.

The sand goby is another type of fish that must be supplied with egg-attaching material. It lays its eggs on a smooth, broad surface. Split sections of bamboo with the septae removed, broad leaves, or the broad stalk of a palm leaf may be used to induce spawning. These are set below the water with the smooth surface facing downward (the fish attach their eggs from underneath) in areas where the fish prefer to lay eggs.

HORMONE TREATMENT: Some fish can be induced to spawn only by the injection of sexual hormone or pituitary gland extract. Not only are such fish (e.g. grass, silver, snail, bighead, and bottom carps) given this treatment, but it is also applied as an additional aid to fish that can be spawned without much difficulty. The technique of using hormones to induce ovulation was first used by animal husbandrists and subsequently by aquarium fish breeders. The method was simplified and made available to the food fish industry about 15 years ago, when it was widely popularized. Using hormone treatment, it has been possible to spawn many fish successfully, including those that had heretofore failed to spawn under controlled conditions. Chinese and Indian major carps, the grey mullet, Siamese *Pangasius* catfish, *Clarias* catfish, the snakehead, and the *Puntius* carp are among those fish that have been spawned recently using this method. Injection of hormones into fish has been standardized and is now applied on a large scale in Southeast Asia.

Although people can successfully induce fish to spawn by the application of hormones, many facts about the physiology of fish reproduction and the biological basis of the hormonal action are still incompletely understood. The pituitary gland of a donor of the same species of fish as the recipient has proven the best hormonal substance for that species. To induce a Chinese major carp to spawn, we use the pituitary gland of another Chinese major carp. The pituitary gland of the common carp has proven useful in spawning many kinds of fish, and the common carp is known as a "universal donor." Usually the more closely a fish is related to the recipient phylogenetically, the better the donor it will be. It is also possible to buy commercial products; HCG (human chorionic gonadotrophin) has proven very useful in inducing many fish to spawn.

Let us review the induced spawning technique used on Chinese carp, as it is quite similar to that used on other fish. Selection of mature fish by examination of morphological characters and stage of ovarian maturation is followed by segregation of males from females. Most Chinese major carps require 2-3 years to mature, but the best brood stock are 3-4-year-olds. Pituitary glands are usually obtained from fish on sale in the market; good fish are seldom sacrificed for gland extraction. In Southeast Asian food markets many different kinds of live or freshly killed fish are sold year-round. Arrangements can usually be made with the fish seller to extract the gland at small cost without buying the whole

fish. Formerly the pituitary gland was extracted by severing the head from the fish, removing the upper part of the cranium to expose the brain, and lifting the brain to remove the now-exposed pituitary resting in a depression underneath. This technique was frowned on by fish sellers, for in Asia fish are almost always sold alive, or at least whole; a fish without a head is not desired. The method now practiced involves using a special drill to bore into the fish head from above through the cranium. A small core is removed which contains the gland. The resulting hole is scarcely noticeable. The pituitary gland can either be used immediately or preserved for later use in alcohol or acetone.

Before injection the glands are ground up thoroughly in a small tissue homogenizer, and dilutant (either distilled water or saline solution) is added to make up the desired amount. HCG or a synthetic hormone (e.g. Synorhorin) may be used in combination with the pituitary gland substance to increase spawning efficiency. In tropical fish, two injections are usually applied to the female fish—an initial injection followed 12 hours later by the final injection. Injections are given intramuscularly above the lateral line between the scales. After the second injection, the fish are watched continuously for signs of readiness to spawn or to be stripped. If the water temperature is high and the fish are active, they may be ready for spawning 4-5 hours after injection, or it may take 12, 15, or 20 hours. One of the signs of readiness is distension of the female fish's belly and corresponding weight increase. When it has been determined that the fish are ready to spawn, they are stripped and artificial fertilization is performed, or they are released into the spawning pond and allowed to spawn naturally. Stripping assures the obtaining of eggs, but involves a considerable danger of injuring the parent fish. Natural spawning is safe for the parent fish but does not guarantee results. Both methods are usually tried.

Following spawning, the incubation of eggs, hatching, and care of the hatchlings are part of a hatchery's operations. In Southeast Asia, hatcheries are extremely simple; it is possible to construct a hatchery capable of producing over 10 million fry annually for less than $50,000. The hatchery is usually a simple building or hut (weather is mild year-round) sheltering several pairs of incubation, hatching, and fry troughs, each approximately 20-30 feet long, 4-5 feet wide, and 2-3 feet deep. Fertilized eggs are placed in conical nets suspended in these troughs so that the water level reaches halfway up the nets. A gentle, slow flow of water is maintained through the nets. Rubber hoses attached to faucets placed beneath the nets provide upward currents of water that keep the eggs in continuous slow motion and oxygenate the water. Eggs of most of the major carps usually hatch within 24 hours; common carp eggs take 2-3 days. The shortest incubation period is that of the kissing gourami—16 hours. Eggs are seldom infested with fungi or other infections because of the short incubation period, a special advantage to Southeast Asian fish culture. Larvae may be kept in the hatching nets for 2-3 days until their yolk is fully absorbed before being transferred to fry nets, fry troughs, or small fry ponds called baby ponds. These baby ponds or nursery ponds are heavily fertilized and shallow (water is less than 1 foot deep); water is kept flowing in them very slowly. Sunlight filtering through stimulates the growth of green algae, plankton, small crustaceans, and worms. The addition of manure encourages the growth of protozoans, ciliates, rotifers, and minute crustaceans such as copepods, (Cyclops), Daphnia, and Moina, all excellent food for fish fry and larvae. When this natural food is not sufficient, or in cases where the youngsters cannot utilize it effectively, wheat flour, rice flour, peanut and soybean cake flours, rice bran, wheat bran, crushed hard-boiled egg yolk, or soybean milk are added to the pond. Young eels, which become carnivorous early, are often fed a special diet that includes crushed clams and trash fish. Within 2 weeks to 1 month, the fry have become fingerlings large enough to transfer to the fish farmers' grow-out ponds.

For short distances fry are still transported as they were long ago, in wide, shallow bamboo baskets hung on poles carried over the shoulder. The baskets are coated with Tung oil (a plant oil) and layered with coated paper to make them waterproof. They are filled with 2-3 inches of water; the natural agitation caused by human locomotion provides enough mechanical aeration to keep the fry alive. For longer distances the fry are put into plastic bags inflated with oxygen. Several days before the journey the fry are conditioned by periodically being driven into a small area to accustom them to crowding. One to two days immediately before packing, feeding is ceased and the fishes' stomachs are allowed to empty. Waste material from full stomachs would soon pollute the water in the plastic bag, depleting the oxygen supply. Long ago, millions of fry were transported from the interior of mainland China through Hongkong to Southeast Asia in large wooden tubs on board ships. Each tub was managed day and night by a worker whose job it was to continuously churn the water with a simple cross bar to keep the water well aerated. Upon arrival at their destination, the fry were transferred into conditioning ponds, then into nursery ponds to grow to fingerling size for sale to fish farmers.

5 Culturing Facilities

Fish farmers in Southeast Asia use almost anything that is both economical and simple to culture their fish, although production is correspondingly lower than that based on elaborate techniques or equipment. A balance must always be struck between cost of input and realized profits. Extensive acreage may be farmed to offset the smaller yields per unit area. Most of the methods of aquaculture I will describe are those rural people use to economically produce fish, usually to be sold at prices within reach of the masses. Milkfish, a typical example of an economically produced fish, are sold at $.30/lb to the consumers. Luxury items, such as eels, may be sold at $5/lb, while live shrimp are sold in Japan for $10-$15/lb.

Many kinds of fish-culturing facilities are found in fresh, brackish, and marine environments. Fish are grown in ponds, lakes, water reservoirs, swamps, ricefields, pens, corrals, baskets, cages or nets.

Ponds

Most fish are cultured in ponds in Southeast Asia. The pond is usually made of mud or earth, with low, narrow embankments similar to those in an Asian ricefield. Ponds are predominantly constructed in low-productive areas or wastelands, such as flooded lowlands that cannot be used for agricultural purposes, temporary reservoirs in flooded valleys, marshes, swamps, estuarine flats, mangrove swamps, farm water reservoirs, burrowed pits (dug to obtain soil for highway construction), and poor rice land. A few hundred years ago Bangkok was a mangrove swamp; its water table remains very near the surface. When residents wanted to construct houses, they first had to dig up a portion of their land as fill. The resulting pit was used as a multipurpose pond for bathing, cleaning food, and growing fish. For this reason almost every family in Bangkok has a fish pond. In Malaysia, where extensive tin mining has

taken place, the resulting pits called "mining pools" are also used for fish culture.

Where it is necessary to excavate a pond, the people never dig very deep; not only is it too expensive, but it wastes valuable top soil. Four to five inches of rich topsoil are first removed and put aside. A second layer 1 foot deep is removed and used to construct a dike 2-3 feet high all around the pond. The layer of topsoil is then replaced over the pond bottom as a source of nutrients. Most ponds are constructed by human labor; only recently have machines such as bulldozers been used to assist in clearing trees, excavating the land, and leveling. Cement ponds are rarely found since they are costly to construct and poor in natural production of food organisms. However, if fish having burrowing habits such as the catfish or common carp are cultured, wood planks, bricks, or small stones are used to line the embankments. Fruit trees and shrubs together with some suitable cover crops may be planted along the sides and around the top of the pond as protection against bank erosion, and the former may even be a source of additional income.

The shape of a pond generally conforms to the topography of the land; convenience and economy are prime factors of consideration. Whenever possible, ponds are built in a rectangular shape for ease of operation (especially harvesting with seine nets). Sizes of ponds range from less than 0.1 acre (most of the catfish ponds in Thailand) to over 500 acres (some of the milkfish ponds in the Philippines). The average pond is 1-5 acres in size and is managed by a single family. A large family usually farms a number of small ponds rather than a few larger ponds. Milkfish ponds are usually greater in area than other types of fish ponds. Vast ponds, such as those found in the Philippines, usually occur in remote, poorly populated areas.

Nursery ponds are generally 0.5 to 1.0 foot deep, fingerling ponds 1-2 feet deep, and grow-out ponds 4-5 feet deep, although in the case of floodlands or reservoirs, they may be more than 10 feet deep. Adult fish, such as the milkfish, that prefer shallow water, may be grown in ponds only 1-2 feet deep. Ponds over 10 feet deep are not only more expensive to excavate but are relatively poor in the production of food organisms.

Most fish ponds in Southeast Asia are "stagnant" as a result of very slight water flow. In many of the heavily fertilized ponds, a strong current would leach out too many nutrients. A balance must be struck between loss of fish food and adequate aeration. Rapid water flow is usually maintained in ponds where fish are being held in high densities.

Most freshwater ponds are dug where there is an adequate supply of water either from streams or rivers. Some ponds rely on rain during the rainy season as a source of water. These ponds are made deeper to retain enough water to last through the dry season. Water may also be supplied by underground sources, artesian wells, water reservoirs, or irrigation systems.

Brackish-water ponds are built along coastal estuarine areas, but never facing the sea directly. They are usually found along tidal canals at least 50-100 yards away from the shoreline as protection against wind and waves. Sluice gates are built along these tidal canals, which serve as a source of sea water. Ponds may also be built in estuarine areas where a good supply of brackish water can be obtained once or twice a day from natural tidal action. A reliable supply of fresh water must also be available, especially during the dry season or in ponds where there is limited water interchange. Evaporation rates are extremely rapid in the tropics, often raising the salinity in a pond to 40 or 50°/00. Not only fish, but fish food such as algae diatoms, are highly sensitive to salinity.

The simplest ponds in Southeast Asia are trapping-holding-growing ponds, built alongside rivers with small water gates to allow entry of fish. When the gates are closed, the trapped fish are either taken out and used immediately, or allowed to grow there. This primitive type of pond is becoming rarer but is still in existence.

Another type of pond is the general multipurpose pond. It may belong to a single family, or more often to a community. It is used to wash clothing, household articles, kitchen utensils, rice and vegetables, as well as to grow fish. Many communities have such a pond, and when the fish are harvested, usually at New Year or some other important occasion, they are distributed among the families of the community. Real fish farms consist of several common types of ponds: the brood stock pond, segregation pond, spawning and hatching ponds, nursery ponds for fry and fingerlings, and grow-out ponds for the final step in the culturing process. In subtropical areas like Taiwan, an additional "wintering" pond is used. This pond is long, narrow, and approximately 5-6 feet deep; the added depth serves as protection from the weather and aids in retention of warmth from the earth. Racks are constructed along the side of the pond and covered with straw to obstruct the cold north wind, while allowing sun from the south to warm the water. Those tropical fish that cannot survive the 2 to 3 months of cold winter are held in the wintering pond until spring, when they are re-released into the grow-out ponds.

Lakes and Water Reservoirs

Lakes and water reservoirs are now used to a large extent in fish culture in Southeast Asia. It has been only since World War II, with the large-scale construction of dams and reservoirs for generation of electricity and irrigation, that more extensive use of these has been made. Since reservoirs and small lakes cannot be managed as carefully or fertilized as efficiently as smaller ponds, fish are stocked in them in lower densities. Larger-growing fish are usually used since they can be caught more easily than smaller species. Many reservoirs are stocked and managed jointly by the local residents and the government; harvests are shared according to prearranged agreement. The stocking of edible, fast-growing organisms has proven to be a valuable way of increasing protein production in Southeast Asian countries where these small bodies of water are abundant.

Swamps, Marshes, Mangroves

There are numerous swamps, marshes, and mangroves in Southeast Asia where dense shrubs and thickets enclose wild, primitive jungle. Many of these areas have been cleared, leveled, deepened, and diked. The creation of a good water supply and drainage system has completed the conversion of these areas into excellent fish ponds.

Ricefields

Rice is a staple food of Southeast Asians, and ricefields are found everywhere. These fields are usually 1-4 acres in size and are plowed with the help of animals. Four to five inches of standing water is almost always present in the well-fertilized field. From time immemorial, farmers observed that many kinds of fish lived in the ricefields. Fingerlings and fish eggs entered with incoming water through the irrigation canals and grew rapidly on the rich supply of algae, rotifers, crustaceans, worms, insects, and other food thriving there. The ricefield thus served as a simple trapping-holding-growing pond. If the bunds of the ricefield are strengthened, water can be held at higher levels and for a longer period of time, creating conditions suitable for fish stocking.

In paddy-cum-fish farming (rice grown with fish), farmers may first plant rice in the field and let water fill it to the proper depth. When the rice seedlings are rooted, fingerlings of the desired species are then stocked. Stocking of fish may also be done passively by the natural process of allowing fingerlings from the irrigation canal to enter the field. In other types of paddy-cum-fish farming, the ricefield may be converted into a fish pond (and utilized solely for fish culture) for the 3-month period of rest usually taken between the two crops of rice grown annually. (Each crop of rice takes 4 months.) Crops of rice and fish may also be regularly alternated for given periods of time. Lastly, a ricefield may be wholly converted to fish culture when it is not very productive. Since the price of fish is rising much more rapidly than the price of rice, this has become a more frequent occurrence lately. Catfish farming in the United States began in ricefields and within a short period of about 15 years grew to a multimillion dollar industry involving thousands of acres of land and farm reservoirs converted into ponds.

Pens and Corrals

Another type of facility used for fish culture is the pen or corral, found primarily in lagoons or lakes. Nylon netting of specific mesh sizes wrapped around bamboo frames is used to enclose the culture areas. The netting allows phytoplankton and other small food organisms to enter freely with the water; oxygen content is the same within and without the enclosure. The only expenses involved are the construction of the corral and the price of the stocked fish.

Cages and Baskets

In the more remote riverside villages of Thailand and Indonesia, bamboo baskets of various sizes are partially submerged in rivers. Branches are inserted in the baskets and soon are covered with a thick growth of epiphytes and various types of algae, which harbor protozoans, worms, and a number of other small animals. Small fish enter the baskets and grow there, feeding on the rich food found among the branches. This form of basket culture is becoming rarer, but can still be found.

There are many types of cages used for aquaculture. They are usually made of bamboo, rattan, wood planks and, less frequently of wire or nylon netting. These cages can be set along rivers, in streams, or along the edges of lakes and lagoons. In brackish water they are placed in tidal canals or other estuarine areas. Cages are also used in bays, coves, and similar marine environments sheltered from wind and wave.

6 Aquaculture Practices and Techniques: Introduction

Acre for acre, water can produce greater amounts of protein food in the form of fish than land can produce of animal protein and can do it more economically. Living in a fluid medium and being cold-blooded, fish need not spend as much energy as land animals in supporting their body weight or keeping their body temperatures constant. Spending much less energy on vital maintenance activities than land animals, they can direct more of their food energy into growth. Yet while animal husbandry has already grown to a state where wild stocks are rarely hunted for food, the major part of world fisheries is still dependent on hunting or capture operations.

There are many ways to define the objectives of fish culture. I think we can say fairly safely that the objective of aquaculture is to produce the maximum quantity of high quality, marketable fish through the most economical management measures possible. Within the context of the very simple economies of Southeast Asia, this means: (1) utilizing solar energy to an optimum degree; (2) utilizing as much agriculturally unproductive space (surface area) as possible, since extensive mechanization or building upward (the sky-scraper concept) is yet not economically feasible; (3) utilizing food organisms produced naturally in the ponds rather than artificial feeds; (4) growing noncarnivorous fish or invertebrates such as mussels or clams, with the exception of luxury items; (5) combining the various types of fish that utilize different foods into an effective polyculture system.

There is always an upper limit to the amount of fish that can be produced in a given pond, no matter how well managed. The fish-carrying capacity of a pond is determined mainly by the amount of fish food available, and the physical-chemical-biological characteristics of the water. With proper techniques and good management, water conditions can be improved and food increased to dramatically raise the natural production of fish. In any kind of aquaculture operation, the following basic steps are involved; how well they are carried out will determine the success of the venture: (1) procurement of stocking material; (2) preparation of culturing facility; (3) maintenance of good culturing conditions (e.g. water quality); (4) manipulation of stocking and growing fish populations to produce the maximum amount of fish for the least expense; (5) food and feeding (that which can be produced in the pond [natural food], and supplemental food introduced from outside); (6) control of pests, predators, and parasites; (7) harvesting; (8) marketing; (9) economy of operation.

We can group the types of aquaculture found in Southeast Asia today into two artificial categories: Natural Stocking and Controlled Stocking.

Natural Stocking

TRAPPING-HOLDING-GROWING PONDS. These are the most primitive type of culturing facility; the main job is construction of a proper embankment at a suitable location.

SIMPLE POND OPERATION. In this category some effort is made to provide control of inflow and outflow and to make the pond more habitable for the cultured organism. Good examples are the shrimp ponds of Singapore. These ponds are constructed in brackish-water areas, originally mangrove swamps. Water enters from a tidal canal, and young fish, shrimps, and other organisms are allowed to enter naturally with the high tide. Later this water inflow is closed off with some sort of sluice gate. The soil in these ponds is rich enough to support a large quantity of natural food organisms for the shrimps; 200-400 lbs of shrimp/acre/annum are commonly produced.

RICEFIELD FISH CULTURE. Stocking material from natural sources enters the ricefield with the incoming water.

Controlled Stocking

In this type of culture, water is allowed to enter the pond while most naturally occurring organisms can be kept out. The farmer controls the kinds, numbers, and times when cultured animals are stocked. Simple ponds in which the natural stocking method is used can be converted to this type simply by the construction of more elaborate water gates to keep undesirable organisms, such as carnivorous predators, out.

MONOCULTURE. The culture of a single species. Maximum production of a carnivorous fish monoculture pond without application of fertilizer and without feeding, is about 100-200 lb/acre/annum. If nothing is done to the pond but switch it to a form of noncarnivorous fish culture, at least twice as many fish can be produced. If fertilizer is added to the pond, production can be boosted to 600-800 lb/acre/annum. When supplemental feed is also added, production may reach 1,000-3,000 lb/acre/annum. In such forms of high-intensity culture, there are the constant dangers of oxygen depletion, waste material toxicity, or a number of other reductions in water quality. In these ponds water flow adequate to ensure water quality while at the same time slight enough to retain fertilizer and other food material is maintained. Typical examples of controlled stocking monoculture are the culture of tilapia, milkfish, freshwater eels, and catfish.

POLYCULTURE. This may involve culturing together different species of fish with compatible food habits, or the culture of fish with shrimps or other invertebrates, provided the fish is not a predator of the other cultured organism(s).

FISH CULTURE INTEGRATED WITH AGRICULTURE OR ANIMAL HUSBANDRY. This may involve: (1) Vegetable gardening using "aquatic vegetables" such as water spinach or water chestnuts in the pond. (2) Land vegetables grown on banks of the pond. (3) Sugar cane grown between ponds. (4) Fish culture integrated with silkworm production. Mulberry trees whose leaves are used to feed silkworms are grown between ponds, while silkworm droppings serve as fertilizer and silkworm pupae are used to feed the fish. (5) Fruit trees such as bananas, papayas, or coconuts are grown between ponds. (6) Integration with chicken or pig farming. Droppings become fertilizer for ponds, either directly or after being collected and disinfected. Water weeds from the pond are used for feeding the pigs and chickens. (7) Integration with duck raising. Ducks are confined to one area of the pond, and droppings serve as fertilizer. Duck eggs and ducks for the table may be harvested, in addition to fish.

I would like to discuss how the basic principles of aquaculture are applied in each of the types of fish culture I have mentioned. In the following chapters I will discuss the pond culture of tilapia, milkfish, walking catfish, snakehead, and the freshwater eel, as well as examples of pen culture, cage and basket culture, ricefield culture, polyculture, fish culture integrated with agriculture and animal husbandry, and crustacean culture.

7 Tilapia Culture

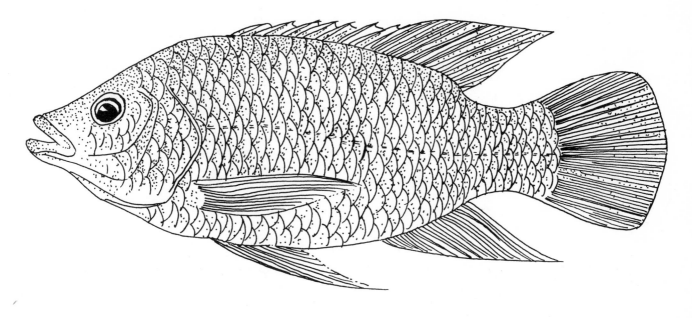

ILLUSTRATION 2.　　　　　　　　　　Tilapia　　　　*Tilapia mossambica* (Peters)

Tilapia mossambica, within a short period of about 35 years, has from obscurity come to be the most commonly known fish and the most important pond-cultured species, as far as production is concerned, in Southeast Asia. It is a fish native to Africa. Because of its fascinating mouth-breeding habit and some interesting markings on its body, it was imported to Asia as an exotic aquarium fish. Evidently, some of those imported into Indonesia escaped from the aquarium and established themselves in some pools. They were not noticed until 1939 when their presence was first discovered by Mr. Mudjia, a fish culture extension officer of the Fisheries Service of the Indonesian Government. Mr. Mudjia

was later honored by his government when they named this fish "Ikan Mudjia" (*Ikan* means fish in Indonesian). Since there were many excellent fish already being extensively cultured in Indonesia, this newly discovered foreign fish was not given much attention until the arrival of the Japanese occupation army.

As soon as the war broke out, many of the coastal areas where milkfish fry abound were declared prohibited areas to all fishermen and fish fry collectors because of their military importance. The supply of milkfish fry was suddenly greatly decreased. To help solve the serious shortage of milkfish fry, stocking tilapia in brackish-water ponds was tried and was found to be satisfactory. Stocking of tilapia in the thousands of hectares of idle milkfish ponds was then strongly encouraged by Japanese occupation authorities. It worked so well that within a few years tilapia had spread all over Indonesia. From Indonesia they were introduced into Singapore and Malaya, from there to Thailand, and from Thailand to Hongkong, the Philippines, Vietnam, Cambodia, and Laos. In 1946, thirteen specimens of *T. mossambica* were brought to Taiwan from Singapore by Chen-huei WU and Chi-hsin KUO. Thousands of millions of offspring have been produced, and today tilapia are the most common and most important pond fish of this island. In honor of Wu and Kuo, tilapia is known as "Wu-Kuo" fish in Taiwan.

Today, it is found in virtually every kind of water—ponds, ditches, canals, reservoirs, ricefields, etc.—in many parts of Southeast Asia in great abundance. It is a blessing in areas where people are in urgent need of cheap protein food or where they appreciate eating fish of small size, but it may become a nuisance in places where many good food fish are already being extensively cultured, especially on milkfish farms where tilapia are liable to destroy the all-important source of milkfish food—the benthic algal mat. However, it is an established fact that tilapia is now an important low-priced food fish for the people of Southeast Asia.

Some of the good characteristics of tilapia, however, can cause problems. Tilapia are able to reproduce when only about 5-6 months old and can breed once in about every two months, provided the range of water temperature is between 26-32° C. As a result, a pond soon becomes overpopulated, and very often all the fish become stunted and remain tiny in size. To help control the problem of overpopulation, the following methods have been tried: (1) introduction of faster growing and less prolific species, (2) introduction of suitable local predatory fish, (3) monosex culture, and (4) culture of selected hybrids.

Species such as *T. zillii, T. melanoplura, T. hornorum,* and *T nilotica* have been introduced on a trial basis. When they were cultured alone, no significant improvement was shown. Using predatory fish to control population of tilapia requires careful manipulation and control of stocking and pond management.

Monosex culture is based on the fact that when only one sex of fish is cultured, no reproduction is possible and material and energy normally used for reproduction are used instead for the growth of the individual fish. Young males and females over 1.5 months old can usually be separated on the basis of differences in the structure of the genital papillae. However, the process of sexing is laborious and it is difficult to obtain an accuracy of over 95%. The presence of just one female fish in a pond stocked with males is enough to spoil the entire monosex culture operation. Another method of obtaining specimens for monosex culture is the crossing of two suitable species of tilapia. In Southeast Asia, over 95% male offspring have been produced by:

♂ *T. mossambica* X ♀ *T. nilotica*
♂ *T. hornorum* X ♀ *T. mossambica*

The use of hybrid tilapia for culture is gaining popularity rapidly. Among the hybrids, the one that has shown the best characteristics—faster growth rate and ability to grow to larger size—is produced from ♂ *T. nilotica* X ♀ *T. mossambica;* it is now being extensively cultured in Taiwan.

Common Tilapia Culture Method

WATER CONDITIONS AND POND PREPARATION. Tilapia are the easiest fish to culture. They can be cultured in almost any kind of pond, fresh water or brackish water, seasonally or permanently. They prefer fertile ponds, with loamy soil and about 2-3 feet of water. The usual procedures of preparing a pond for stocking of fish in Southeast Asia are followed. Organic materials such as cow-dung, pig-dung, chicken manure, green compost/manure, etc. are used as fertilizers.

STOCKING PRACTICES. Nonhybridized fry and fingerlings can easily be obtained from one's own or neighbor's grow-out ponds. Hybrids are supplied by government hatcheries or sold by special private fish farms. Stocking is done in early spring or when the water temperature reaches 24° C; either 6,000-10,000 one-inch fingerlings or about 100 pairs of mature fish are stocked per one acre of water area.

FEED. When needed, inexpensive material available locally such as rice bran, coconut meal, peanut cake, soybean cake, chopped trash fish, duck weed, etc. may be used as supplemental feed. In a well-fertilized pond, especially one that is given an ample amount of animal manure daily, very little, if any, supplemental feeding is necessary.

HARVESTING. Mature nonhybridized fish will start spawning within ten days after being introduced into a pond, and the offspring will reach maturity within 6 months. To avoid overpopulation and stunting, a partial harvest should be started 6-7 months after the date of stocking, to remove the large fish for the market. If necessary, young ones can be removed for stocking in other ponds or for other purposes. Partial harvest can be repeated once every month thereafter.

In monoculture of hybrids, young fingerlings are primarily stocked. Since they do not reproduce readily, such fingerlings grow at an even rate and take about 6-7 months to reach good market size. A partial harvest is done about 6 months after stocking and is repeated whenever there is a sign of overcrowding. A complete harvest is done at the end of the culture season.

Other Tilapia Culture Methods

Integration with poultry-and-pig-raising is gaining popularity. Chicken droppings and pig manure, after proper treatment, are used extensively to fertilize the ponds. It is believed that about 20-30% of the pig manure introduced into the pond is taken directly as food by the fish. Tilapia culture in combination with duck raising is also being commonly practiced (in Taiwan). Nonhybridized *T. mossambica* have been cultured with snakehead fish, mainly as food for the latter (see the section on snakehead culture). In the highly productive polyculture system, tilapia is fast becoming one of the principal fish used.

43

8 Milkfish (Chanos chanos) Culture

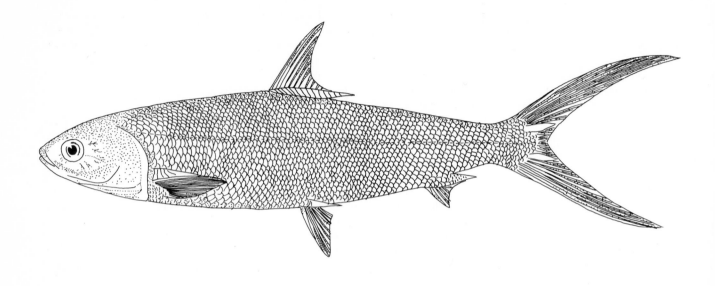

The most important brackish-water pond monoculture in Southeast Asia is that of the milkfish, *Chanos chanos*. The milkfish, so called because of its silvery scales, is present in the tropical waters of the Indian and Pacific oceans and the seas around Southeast Asia, where it is known by many regional names: Taiwan—Sat-Bak-Hi (tiny eye fish); Indonesia and Malaysia—Bandeng; Philippines—Bangas; Hawaii—Awa-awa; Ceylon (Sri Lanka) and India—Palai meen; and Australia—white mullet. Although the milkfish possesses many small bones, its flesh is very tasty, and it is highly regarded in those countries where people are adept at eating bony fish. Mature milkfish (3-4 feet long, 15-20 pounds) are caught occasionally but only in small num-

bers, and have never constituted an important high seas fishery. However, their culture for consumption has been important in Southeast Asia for many years, and eventually its importance may extend to other areas of the globe, not only as a food industry, but as a bait industry for deep-sea fishing.

History

Indonesia, the Philippines, and Taiwan are the world's leaders in milkfish farming. It is generally believed that this industry was started in Indonesia some 500 years ago and was introduced to the Philippines and Taiwan during the 16th century. In Taiwan, milkfish farming was already practiced during the reign of General Cheng Cheng-kung (Koxinga). Undoubtedly, some special socioeconomic factors played important roles in the development of wild coastal swampy jungle areas for large-scale fish farming. It is not unreasonable to believe that many of the early pioneers in milkfish farming in Indonesia were prisoners or enemies of the government) exiled to remote and venomous animal-infested mangrove swamps. Because of the necessity of fighting for survival, they may have learned to obtain food from the jungle, by clearing the mangrove to trap fish (one of the common fish of those mangrove areas is milkfish). After many years of gradual improvement, this led to the development of milkfish farming.

Milkfish Fry

Adult milkfish are occasionally seen in small groups, playing in shallow waters off small, quiet islands, within 1-2 miles from shore. We assume that they spawn in these secluded spots, releasing their semi-floating eggs, but no one has seen them spawn or actually knows where they do so. Although it is known that females can produce 2-3 million eggs, it is probable that very few of these survive to maturity. It is quite possible that the eggs hatch within 24 hours and the yolk-sac larvae are carried by wind and current to coastal areas within 2-3 days. By this time the yolk has been absorbed, and the larvae begin entering brackish or freshwater areas. It is from these coastal and estuarine waters, mangrove areas, and coastal swamps that fry for stocking have traditionally been collected.

Procurement of Stocking Material

Collecting is usually done by children, fishermen's wives, or older men using simple hand nets that do not require strength. For larger scale collection, a seine net with a cod end of fine mesh is dragged through the water. The cod end is protected by a floating basket with an open top through which the collector can periodically reach in and remove fry. In this way the fry are kept from being crushed against the net. Lures may be used to attract fry in a different method of collecting. Milkfish fry tend naturally to hide in seaweeds or other bushy material. Collectors set long ropes, to which are attached bundles of palm leaves, in shallow coastal waters or estuarine areas. Each rope may attract several hundred fry. When the "lure" has been laid for several hours, the fishermen take one end of the rope (the water is only knee-deep) and slowly wind it in concentric circles, driving the fry into the center area. This technique is very popular in Indonesia. In other areas techniques such as setting barrier nets across river mouths to intercept entering fry may be used.

Every year over five billion fry are needed for the three major milkfish-culturing countries (Indonesia, Taiwan, Philippines). This affords numerous employment opportunities for unskilled laborers. It has been speculated that within 5-10 years over seven billion fry will be required. However, there is a limit to the supply of fry that can be collected from nature. Coastal industrialization and rising pollution have already resulted in reduced numbers of naturally occurring fry. The milkfish is one of the few cultured pond fish that has not yet been spawned in captivity or even raised to maturity in ponds. There are several reasons for the latter: (1) older milkfish require deeper water than that commonly used in milkfish ponds; and (2) milkfish reach marketable size within 1 year, while 5-6 years are required for them to reach maturity. The Southeast Asian fish farmer cannot afford to keep milkfish that long, and ponds owned by governmental agencies for experimental purposes often experience changeover of personnel within that period of time.

Presently, several national, regional, and international agencies have begun long-term projects for the development of milkfish culture in Southeast Asia. In Taiwan and the Philippines, projects involving the raising of milkfish to maturity have been initiated. Efforts are being expended to catch mature fish at sea, tranquilize them, inject hormones, and induce the females to release their eggs. As of now, male and female specimens of the proper maturational stage have not been captured at the same time.

Food

The milkfish is basically herbivorous, and is believed to thrive on the filamentous algae, blue-green algae, and diatoms commonly found in a milkfish pond, or on rocks and seabeds of shallow waters. In addition, it ingests tiny crustaceans, worms, protozoans, and rotifers living in the benthic blue-green algal mat at the pond bottom.

FILAMENTOUS ALGAE. These plants, commonly quite coarse in texture, are found floating at the top of the pond. They are very poor nutritionally, and though they may be ingested, cannot be digested by the milkfish. However, when dead, decaying, and soft, they can be adequately utilized by the milkfish. The two common types found in Southeast Asian milkfish ponds are Enteromorpha and Chaetomorpha. These grow rapidly at salinities well above or below the desired range of 20-26°/00.

BLUE-GREEN BENTHIC ALGAE. This is the most important plant group in milkfish culture. Forming a mat at

the pond bottom, it is the major component of the milkfish diet. In the Philippines this benthic algal mat is known as "lab-lab," a term that is gaining common usage. "Lab-lab" consists mainly of blue-green algae of the following types:

Cynophyceae:	Spirulina	Lyngbia*
	Microcoleus	Anabaena*
	Anthrospira	Oscillatoria*

* Cosmopolitan species

DIATOMS. Diatoms may be found in the water or growing within the algal mat. They are useful as food for the milkfish and are easily digested. Commonly found diatoms include Nitzschia, Navicula, Amphora, and Amphiprora.

The milkfish is a tropical marine fish with a wide range of tolerance to salinity; it can be cultured in brackish, marine, or fresh water. In the few countries where milkfish has been cultured, large areas are farmed. (See Table 4.)

Note that although Taiwan suffers a 3-month period of cold weather during which milkfish do not grow, production per unit area is markedly higher there than in Indonesia or the Philippines. This is due to differences in the culturing techniques practiced and the degree of skill used in pond management. The technique and management of milkfish culture involve several

TABLE 4.

ANNUAL MILKFISH PRODUCTION IN SOUTHEAST ASIA

COUNTRY	AREA CULTIVATED (hectares)[A]	ANNUAL TOTAL (metric tons)	PRODUCTION KILOGRAMS/ HECTARE/YEAR (average)	(poorest-best)	GROWING SEASON
Indonesia	184,000	50,000	400	300-1,500	Year-round
Philippines	170,000	90,000	600	350-2,000	Year-round
Taiwan	16,700	33,000	2,000	1,500-3,000	9 months
Thailand, Vietnam, Malaysia	4,000	1,600	450	350-1,000	Year-round

Source: Ling, 1973.
A. 1 hectare (ha) = 2.47 acres.

steps as follows: (1) preparation of ponds, (2) maintenance of water conditions, (3) stocking and stock manipulation, (4) production and maintenance of optimum growth of food organisms within pond, (5) supplemental feeding when necessary, (6) control of pests and predators, (7) harvesting.

Pond Characteristics

The size and location of a milkfish pond vary with the local topography and the farmer's preference. In Taiwan, because of the greater management exercised, a milkfish pond ranges from 1-6 hectares in size. In the Philippines ponds may be as large as 100-500 hectares; management and care are less elaborate by necessity.

Figure 3 gives a general idea of the layout of a typical milkfish farm in Taiwan. Part of the community water supply enters through a canal at the head pond (top right). Five to ten farmers usually share the water from this one major canal. The head pond serves as a settling pond. Feeder canals (center) carry water to the various ponds. Young milkfish fry are first introduced into a tiny temporary enclosure, about 10 feet in diameter, known as the "fry pond" (this is popularly used in the Philippines). It has been specially prepared with a good growth of benthic algae, and walled off from the rest of the complex. Water in which the fry were transported is mixed with a small amount of standing water to minimize shock at the time of introduction. The young fry are given refined food for a few days; then the enclosing walls are broken in several places and water is allowed to enter slowly through screens. In several days, when the fry have been sufficiently conditioned, the screens are removed, and the young fry are allowed to enter the nursery pond. They remain here for about a month until they become young fingerlings of about 3 inches; they may then be driven to an intermediate or transition pond (optional) until they reach 4-5 inches. At this size the milkfish are driven into the grow-out ponds, where they are reared to market size. This improved system is used not only in Taiwan, but is steadily gaining popularity in Indonesia and the Philippines. The wintering pond shown in the diagram is unique to Taiwan. Before the end of November all unharvested fish are driven into this area, which is deeper and which is protected with a windbreaker made of plastic sheets or bundles of hay to keep out the cold wind. Frequently 10-20%, and sometimes over 50% (during severely cold winters) of the half-grown fish die during the winter in these wintering ponds.

Pond Preparation

In Taiwan, pond preparation takes place in December, when all the milkfish have been harvested or driven into the wintering ponds. Elsewhere in Southeast Asia, this procedure is carried out on an annual basis or whenever deemed necessary. Mass fish kills are not uncommon during the hot summer season if the pond has not been properly prepared and rested. Excessive accumulation of organic material increases the dangers of oxygen depletion and toxic gas release, especially after sudden heavy rains, when deeper anaerobic layers of pond soil are overturned. The period of pond preparation is also used by the fish farmer to level the pond bottom and repair the bunds, water gates, water supply, and drainage systems.

The pond is first completely drained and allowed to dry for approximately one month until the bottom cracks. This sun drying aids in the mineralization of organic material left at the pond bottom; cracking of the soil allows release of noxious gases and greater penetration of oxygen into the pond bottom.

The pond is then refilled with 4-5 inches of fresh sea water (February in Taiwan) and allowed to sit until the water has slowly evaporated. This process is repeated several times. The sea water brings in nutrients that accumulate at the pond bottom as fertilizer.

The next step (mid-February or spring in Taiwan) consists of spreading fertilizer evenly over the pond bottom. Fertilizers, predominantly organic, may consist of chicken, cow, steer, or pig manure, or even night soil

FIGURE 3.

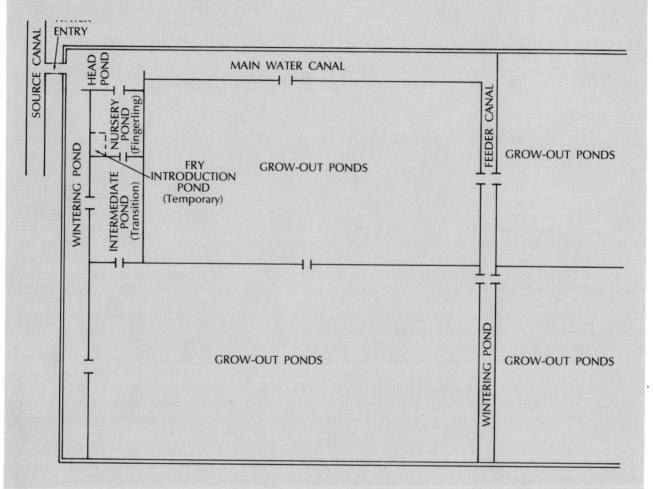

Layout of typical milkfish pond in Taiwan (after Chen, 1952).

48

that has been treated to rid it of parasites. A great deal of rice bran is also used. Water is added to a depth of 3-4 inches, soaking the fertilizer, which is allowed to mineralize and dry up.

Several weeks later, depending on the type of fertilizer used, varying amounts of lime are applied to aid in mineralization of the organic material accumulated at the pond bottom. Heavier applications of lime are used in ponds that have a tendency to become acid (usually those without frequent water interchange). Liming also helps to destroy harmful insect larvae and eggs of predatory and pest fish. Since lime is not a strong enough pesticide, other cheap and readily available materials, such as tea seed cake, are often used. Modern powerful chemical insecticides are rarely applied because they are expensive, dangerous, and the toxic residues are often accumulative. Tea seed cakes are used primarily in Taiwan. They are made from the pressed residues left after oil has been extracted from seeds of the wild tea plant (Camellia) for cooking or hair ointment. Tea seed cakes contain a chemical known as saponin, a potent alkaloi that kills most aquatic insects and many species of fish. This substance reacts with oxygen and water and dissipates within 4-5 days.

In the Philippines tobacco powder is obtained from local tobacco plantations; its effective insecticide ingredient is nicotine. Derris root, the substance from which rotenal is manufactured, grows wild on the mountainsides of most Southeast Asian countries, especially Indonesia. It is used alone or in combination with tobacco powder as a pesticide. The harmful effects of all these pesticides of plant origin usually disappear within 10 days; there does not seem to be any cumulative effect, characteristic of many modern chemical pesticides. The second day after application is the most effective. The insecticides are applied by the end of February or early March in Taiwan and left for 2-3 weeks.

Water is reintroduced into the pond and by late March or early April, about one month later, the pond is ready to receive fry. Although the period of pond preparation spans 2-3 months, much less actual working time is spent. For example, the pond may be worked and filled one day, then left alone 2-3 weeks to dry. During the period of treatment, the pond bottom has become rich in organic material and ideally benthic algae has grown to form a thick green carpet there. This algal mat is the principal source of food for the milkfish, and almost every management practice applied to a milkfish culturing pond is used to promote its growth. The application of fertilizer only to the pond bottom (avoiding dispersion of nutrients into the water) promotes benthic algal growth at the expense of plankton growth. After milkfish have been stocked, additional fertilizer is placed in bags set on the pond bottom from which it can seep into the soil.

Maintenance of Water Conditions

Water is maintained at a level shallow enough to promote benthic algal growth; if the water is too deep, a phytoplankton bloom may result at the surface instead. At the same time, water must be kept deep enough to satisfy the fish. The average depths of ponds are: for small fry, 5-6 inches; for fingerlings (2-3 inches long), 8-12 inches; for grow-out ponds, 2-4 feet. Water flow is maintained at a rate adequate to supply enough oxygen yet not swift enough to leach out valuable nutrients.

Water supply and drainage are very important features of milkfish farms. Since these farms are usually brackish-water ponds, they depend on tidal canals to supply them with water. Individual farms are often located close together and are fed by private feeder canals from a common community canal. The construction and maintenance of the canals and water gates often result in great financial and social problems for the community. In new developing countries there is the danger that ponds may be developed in areas where industrialization will later interfere. A classic example is found in Luzon, where milkfish farms were begun about 200 years ago. The city gradually built up around the farms, and housing developments now prevent adequate drainage during heavy rains. The whole city may remain flooded for several days because the original drainage system is now insufficient.

Optimum salinity range is 20-30°/00 for both the fish and algae. Because of the repeated additions of sea water during the pond preparation period, salinity within the pond may be greater than 32°/00. If possible, fresh water is added to dilute the pond water to a salinity of 25-30°/00. Salinity may rise as high as 50°/00 during the dry season or fall as low as 10°/00 during the rainy season; in these cases either fresh or salt water is pumped in to bring the salinity to the proper level.

The pH is normally maintained at 7.5 to 8; most of the desired algal species do not grow well at pHs below 6.0. In ponds where fresh sea water enters daily, the pH seldom dips below 6.0; in ponds far from the seacoast, lime is often needed to raise the pH.

Fish Stocking and Stock Manipulation

Several fish-stocking methods of varying complexity are used in milkfish culture. Milkfish of the same size may be stocked one or more times a year, depending on their size (single-size stocking). Most frequently very young milkfish (1 gram) are stocked to be harvested at the end of the year. In tropical countries suitable for year-round growth of fish, several crops of larger fingerlings may be stocked and harvested annually, one after another. Fifty-gram milkfish, requiring only 3-4 months to reach market size, are suitable for this practice. Multiple-size stocking involves simultaneous stocking of different-sized fish at the beginning of the season. As fish reach market size, they are harvested. By the time the largest fish are marketable, the smallest fish have grown to an intermediate size, and another group of fry can be introduced. Repeated harvesting and stocking are done throughout the year. At present, multiple-size stocking is popularly used in Taiwan, and is one of the reasons for the higher per acre production rates there.

Production and Maintenance of Food

The production of adequate natural food for milkfish in the culturing pond is crucial to a successful farming operation. The amount of food and the number of fish in the pond must be kept in balance. The procedures involved to do so are more complex with multiple-size stocking but are also more efficient. Let us see why.

Every pond has the capacity to produce a specific amount of benthic algae, and will support only that much until certain conditions (e.g. nutrients, light, turbidity) are altered. This quantity of algae is called the "standing crop" and can be thought of as "capital" in terms of milkfish production. Each day the algae has the ability to replenish itself through growth and reproduction if the standing crop is reduced (e.g. by fish eating it). This daily replenishment capacity is "interest," and the farmer wants the milkfish to utilize it to its fullest extent. A well-managed milkfish pond is one that makes the fullest utilization of the daily yield of fish food from the standing crop without disturbing the standing crop itself. If small amounts are occasionally overdrawn from the standing crop, recovery is possible; but if overdrawn amounts are large and frequent, there is the danger of steadily reducing the size of the standing crop to a point of no return, resulting in complete depletion. Let us examine the relative economy of single-size and multiple-size stocking in terms of algal food production and utilization.

Following are Tables 5, 6, and 7 of figures that we will assume to be characteristic of a 1-hectare milkfish pond and that we will use in the ensuing discussion.

SINGLE-SIZE STOCKING. Let us assume that 6,000 1-gram fish are stocked at the beginning of the season and all are harvested at the end of the year. These young fry

TABLE 5.

BENTHIC ALGAL PRODUCTION IN A 1-HECTARE MILKFISH POND (TAIWAN)

	BEST	(KILOGRAMS)			POOREST
Standing crop	3,500	3,000	2,000	1,000	500
Daily utilizable crop	525	450	300	150	75

TABLE 6.

DAILY FOOD REQUIREMENTS AND GROWTH RATE OF MILKFISH

BODY WEIGHT (grams)	FOOD REQUIREMENT IN PERCENT OF BODY WEIGHT	TIME AFTER STOCKING REQUIRED TO REACH BODY WEIGHT (months)
1	60	0
3	60	1
8	60	2
20	50	3
50	50	4
100	40	5
200	40	6
300[A]	35	7
400[A]	35	

A. Market size.

require 4.8 kg of food daily (8 kg × 60% = 4.8 kg). Looking at Table 5, we see that even our poorest ponds have the capacity to produce 75 kg of algal food daily. Initially a great deal of potentially available food will remain unused. After 3 months our 8,000 fish have grown to 20 grams each, or a total of 160 kg, and will consume 80 kg of algae daily (160 kg × 50%). There is still some wastage of food. When the fish have reached 200 grams in size, after 6 months, they will require 640 kg of food daily (1,600 × 40%). Even our best ponds cannot supply that amount (Table 5), so the fish would naturally feed on the standing crop. If the standing crop of benthic algae is reduced below 1,000 kg, it will not grow back. To save the standing crop from depletion, supplemental feed must be added. In conclusion, one size stocking is uneconomical; at the beginning of the stocking period large quantities of potentially available natural food are wasted, while towards the end of the culturing period, the pond cannot produce enough algae to support the fish. One remedy is to stock larger fish (which consume more food initially) in lesser numbers so that later food demand will be reduced. The technique of multiple-size stocking makes much more efficient use of natural agal production and often results in tremendous gains in amounts of harvested milkfish.

MULTIPLE-SIZE STOCKING. Say we stock 6,000 fry, 2,000 weighing 1 gram, 2,000 weighing 20 grams, and 2,000 weighing 50 grams. This results in a total of 156 kg

TABLE 7.

WEIGHT INCREASE AND CORRESPONDING FOOD DEMAND OF MILKFISH STOCKED IN MULTIPLE SIZES (TAIWAN)

NUMBER OF FRY STOCKED	WEIGHT/FRY (grams)	TOTAL WEIGHT (kilograms)	WEIGHT/FRY AFTER 3 MONTHS (grams)	TOTAL WEIGHT AFTER 3 MONTHS (kilograms)	FOOD DEMAND IN 3 MONTHS (kilograms)
2,000	8	16	100	200 × 40% =	80
2,000	20	40	200	400 × 40% =	160
2,000	50	100	300	600 × 35% =	210
TOTAL 6,000		156		1,200 × 35% =	450

of fish, initially requiring 71 kg of algal food a day. Sixty-five fewer kilograms of food are wasted than in our first example of single-size stocking (5 kg demand initially). At the end of 3 months, each of the fish has grown, resulting in a total demand of 450 kg food/day, an amount most well-managed ponds can supply (Table 5). By now the largest fish have reached market size and can be harvested and replaced with small fish with correspondingly smaller food requirements. Harvesting is usually done four times a year. In a pond where single-size stocking of milkfish is used, maximum production is only 1,000 kg/hectare/annum. However, a well-managed pond in which multiple-size stocking is performed can produce 3,000 kg milkfish/hectare/annum. At the same time, these ponds require a great deal of work; a Taiwanese fish farmer can handle only a 5-hectare pond of such a type working full time. In Indonesia and the Philippines, where single-size stocking is used, culturing areas are commonly as large as 100-500 hectares, but average production is only 500 kg/hectare/annum. Although the milkfish is primarily cultured in brackish water, it can be cultured in fresh water. In the Philippines milkfish are sometimes stocked in small, freshwater lakes to be commercially harvested a year later.

We might ask where the different sizes of milkfish used in multiple-size stocking are obtained. In Taiwan, the first stocking is done in early April with over-wintered fingerlings grown from last year's late fry. The size of these fingerlings ranges from about 10 to 150 g in weight. New fry occur from April through August. New fry are constantly being collected or bought and added to the pond throughout the fry season at intervals of about three to five weeks. While small fry stocked in April, May, and early June can usually be harvested by the time winter arrives, those stocked at the later part of the catching season (late June-August) are too small. All milkfish not large enough to be harvested are driven into the wintering pond. Next year these will be used for multiple-size stocking.

Milkfish are being cultured frequently as bait fish, especially for long-line tuna fishing. Since milkfish have proven excellent as bait when they are only 100 grams in size, the stocking intensity in a pond used for culturing bait can be quite high. More marketable crops can be harvested each year.

There will be times when the natural food supply for the milkfish must be increased or augmented with supplemental feed. Application of fertilizer to increase the algal crop is less expensive than using additional feed, but its efficacy is limited. No matter how much fertilizer is added, the growth rate of the algae has a limiting maximum. During periods of bad weather, such as the typhoon season, when heavy rains dilute the pond water and inhibit the growth of the benthic algae, or when the algal mat becomes infested with worms, insect larvae, chironomids, or snails, the fish farmer must introduce supplemental feed. A similar situation arises shortly before festivals, when the farmers forcefeed the fish to fatten them for the market. Supplemental feed consists of material readily and cheaply available, especially farm byproducts such as rice bran, wheat bran, soybean cake, and peanut cake (the latter two made from the residues left after oil has been extracted). Peanut cake and soybean cake are also fed to pigs and chickens. In the Philippines and Indonesia, copra (the tough, fibrous substance left after coconut oil has been pressed) may be chopped, soaked in water, and fed to the fish. Supplemental feed is usually broadcast over the surface of the pond twice a day.

Control of Pests and Predators

There are many predators and pests in a milkfish pond. The important fish predators include *Elops, Megalops, Theropon, Lates, Epinephalus,* eels, and brackish water marine catfish. Other predators include snakes, lizards, and birds. Fish predators are controlled by preparing and maintaining adequate screens over the water inlets and outlets of the pond. The application of biocide to the pond during the drying period serves to kill any dormant fish eggs that may be lying there. Preventive measures are crucial, for once the predatory fish have entered the pond they are difficult to remove. Any chemicals that would kill these predatory fish would kill the milkfish also. Snakes and lizards are caught with special bamboo or wire traps. Birds are more difficult to deal with. In many Southeast Asian countries, because of political problems, people are not allowed to use firearms. Scarecrow structures and noisemakers are only temporarily effective. Fortunately, with so many ponds in the same area, each farmer suffers small losses. One of the main reasons for the difficulty in initiating the first ponds in a new area is that any predators present will rush to the new ponds and have a field-day.

Various types of nonpredatory pests are also found in milkfish ponds. Tilapia may cause trouble because of their habit of building saucer-shaped nests on the pond bottom, destroying the valuable benthic algal mass. Tilapia propagate rapidly, building new nests every 2-3 months; several dozen of these fish can cover an entire pond bottom with holes. Since the tilapia is so tenacious once it has established itself, the farmers take great care to prevent its introduction into the pond. During the period of pond preparation, drying, liming, and application of pesticides all help to destroy any tilapia eggs that may be present. A very fine screen is used as a water gate to prohibit the entry of fry.

Snails compete with milkfish for algal food. To prevent their propagation, a thick, healthy growth of benthic algae is maintained. Because the snails require a substratum to crawl on, this effectively prohibits their movement and they eventually die, tangled in the algae. Young people may be employed to collect the snails, which will be crushed and used as feed for other organisms, such as snail carp or shrimp. If many snails are present, chemicals may be used; chemicals developed specifically for killing snails are now being tried.

Another pest is the larvae of chironomid midges known as "bloodworms." These occur by the millions, and feed on the lab-lab. Many kinds of insecticides have been employed to eradicate them. A few, such as Dipteryx, were found that left the fish unharmed. However, these chemicals were both expensive and uneconom-

ical. It was discovered that when shrimps (Penaeus monodon and P. japonicus) were introduced into the milkfish pond they fed on the midge larvae and served as effective biological control agents. At harvest time the shrimps can be harvested with the milkfish, often bringing in more money.

The egg mass of a bristleworm (polychaete) may cause problems if abundant. Young fry become entangled in these gelatinous, sticky masses and perish. The egg masses are removed by hand or with small nets, usually by the farmer's children.

Another troublesome animal is the scorpionlike shrimp, Thalassina scorpionidae. It digs deep tunnels as nests into the banks of the pond, often causing leakage. The burrows can be located by searching for fecal pellets deposited around their entrance. Hot water or chemicals, especially those that generate gas, are then poured through a bamboo tube into the burrow to kill the pest.

Harvesting

The time of harvest corresponds with market demand whenever possible. In the Southeast Asian region, many typhoons strike between May and October. Since the fishermen cannot go out to sea, milkfish farmers are able to sell their fish for a much better price. During the large festivals or celebrations quite common in Southeast Asia, fish are always in great demand and fetch high prices.

In the Philippines, Indonesia, or any area where single-size stocking is practiced, harvesting is comparatively simple. The pond may be drained completely and the fish removed singly by hand, or the pond may be drained only half way, and the fish collected with seine nets. In Taiwan, where multiple-size stocking is done, selective harvesting must be performed. First the farmers decide what size fish they want to catch (usually 250-300-gram fish). Then they select a gill net of the proper mesh size. If the farmers are rich, they will have enough of the proper-sized nets; poorer families usually own only a few nets and borrow or rent the remainder from neighbors at harvest time. The nets are joined together and used without prior draining of the pond.

Transportation to Market

Milkfish are usually harvested during periods of warm weather. Asian people are very particular about the freshness of their fish; they do not like them frozen. The farmers try to chill the fish just enough to keep them from spoiling before they reach the market. It is usually a 2-3 hour journey from the fish farm to the market; auctioning in the market lasts 2-3 hours; another 2-3 hours may be taken before the consumer purchases the fish. It is a full 10 hours from the time the fish is first harvested to the time the customer receives it for dressing. Spoilage usually begins with autodigestion in the intestine. Milkfish farmers have devised an ingenious method using the natural habits of the fish to clean their guts without actually cutting and removing them. The milkfish is highly excitable and when excited it not only ceases feeding but also defecates. A

TABLE 8.

PROJECTED ANNUAL PROFIT AND LOSS STATEMENT FOR A 1-HECTARE MILKFISH POND (TAIWAN, 1973)

	NT (New Taiwan dollar)[A]	
REVENUE		
Sale of fish (2,000 kg at NT $24/kg)	$48,000	
Sale of byproducts (crabs, shrimps, etc.)	2,000	
TOTAL SALES		$50,000
EXPENDITURES		
Interest on capital investment	NT $ 6,000	
Equipment	500	
Maintenance and repair	1,500	
Stocking material (fish seed)	12,000	
Feeds	2,000	
Fertilizer and pesticides	8,000	
Wages (labor and management)	9,000	
Miscellaneous	1,000	
TOTAL PRODUCTION EXPENDITURES		$40,000
NET INCOME		NT $10,000 or US $250

Source: Ling's estimate.
A. New Taiwan dollar (NT $40 = US $1).

54

few hours before midnight the farmers scare the milk-fish by drawing a long rope, to which are attached palm fibers and wood boards, across the water. The attached objects flop about, creating a great deal of noise. Two youngsters follow the rope as it is being drawn across the pond and beat the surface of the water with long sticks. In this way the fish are driven from one end of the pond to the other. When they are finally netted, very little food material remains in their intestines.

Milkfish are usually marketed fresh, but surplus produce may be smoked or canned for local or gourmet consumption. About 5 years ago a demand for small milkfish as bait was initiated. The size of the harvested milkfish varies with the use to which it is put:

Human consumption (fresh)	3-4 fish/kg
Human consumption (smoked)	2 fish/kg
Bait	10-12 fish/kg

The cost of production of milkfish is only $.50/kg, or approximately $.24/lb (1973-before energy crisis). Thus it is possible to produce these fish on a large scale for consumption by the common people.

Table 8 shows the estimates of cost and profit of a 1-hectare milkfish pond in Taiwan.

Problems

The most important problem in the development of milkfish culture is the availability of seed. The present annual requirement of fry is in the order of 5 billion, all of which are collected from their natural habitat. The occurrence of fry is unpredictable, and fluctuates widely from year to year and from place to place. In years of scarcity the supply of fry is far below the quantity required, and the price is so high that fish farmers can only afford to have their ponds partially stocked, thus causing increase in production cost and decrease in production.

The problem of maintaining the salinity of the pond water within the favorable range is serious in many localities, especially where there is no reliable supply of fresh water to compensate for the high rate of evaporation during the dry season, or where there is no efficient drainage system to divert rain water from the pond system during the rainy season.

With the improvement of culturing system and pond management, the stocking rate of fish is increasing steadily, demanding more food than the pond is able to produce. The availability of efficient but cheap supplemental feed is becoming a serious problem that requires urgent solution.

9 Walking Catfish (*Clarias batrachus*) Culture

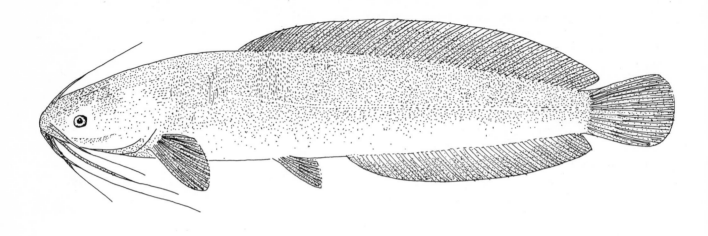

ILLUSTRATION 8.   Clarias catfish   *Clarias batrachus* (L.) (After Arifin)

I shall use catfish culture to illustrate an aquaculture system radically different from that of milkfish. *Clarias* catfish culture was initiated in Thailand only 15 years ago. At that time the building of dams had gradually reduced the swampland which was the fishes' natural habitat. As the numbers of wild catfish steadily diminished, demand spurred the initiation of domesticated culture. *Clarias* catfish culture has since spread to Malaysia, Hongkong, Taiwan, the Philippines, and many other countries. It is characterized by the highest stocking and feeding rates in Southeast Asian fish culture.

Among the various species of *Clarias* cultured in Southeast Asia, *Clarias batrachus* is the most popular, followed by *C. macrocephalus* and *C. fuscus*. *Clarias batrachus* and *C. macrocephalus* are present in most of the Southeast Asian countries, while *C. fuscus* is indigenous to Taiwan. They occur in most stagnant and semi-stagnant fresh waters—shallow lakes, swamps, rain pools, ricefields, and flooded low lands. Possessing an accessory respiratory organ able to make use of atmospheric air directly, they can survive long periods of time out of water in moist areas, or in water having very low dissolved oxygen content. When necessary, they are capable of "walking" across wet fields or land for a short distance with the help of their pectoral fins, especially after a heavy rain. Hence they are sometimes called the "walking" catfish.

These are carnivorous/omnivorous/scavenger fish, feeding on worms, insect larvae, and other small aquatic animals. Often they prefer soft decayed food material.

In tropical waters, these catfish are able to grow to sexual maturity in about 1 year, but would require 1.5 to

2 years in subtropical and temperate waters. Spawning takes place predominantly during the rainy season, but occurs also whenever the water temperature is above 28°C and fresh, well-oxygenated water is available. Elongated holes are made by the fish along the banks or edges of their aquatic habitat to serve as spawning "nests." Eggs are deposited inside these nests, where they adhere to grasses or soil within the hole. These are protected by the parent fish throughout the incubation period and until the young fry are able to feed by themselves.

The commonly cultured species *Clarias batrachus* and the more expensive *Clarias macrocephalus* are grown using similar techniques. Ponds used for catfish culture are very small, usually about 100-400 square meters; the largest I have ever seen was about 1,000 square meters. Water is kept at a depth of 2-3 meters (much deeper than a milkfish or snakehead pond). A sluggish water flow is maintained with water being pumped in from nearby rivers, streams, irrigation canals, or even deep wells if surface water is too polluted with industrial wastes.

Water Conditions and Pond Preparation

In addition to the usual methods and procedures of pond preparation practiced in other kinds of pond fish culture, special attention is given to the strengthening of the bunds to prevent possible escape of catfish by climbing or burrowing. The bunds are built as strong as possible and their inside walls are often lined with bricks or wooden boards or planks. For further protection, most of the ponds are fenced with bamboo or wire screens to a height of about 1.5 feet. Pipes are inserted into the bunds to serve as nests.

Stocking Material and Practices

Stocking material may be collected from natural habitats or produced in ponds. Collection of stocking material is done primarily during the rainy season, in swamps, ricefields, flooded lowlands, etc. Fingerlings are collected with small hand nets and scoop nets and are suitable for stocking in ponds immediately. Small fry are collected from the spawning nests (holes) with small, fine-meshed hand nets, and are reared in nursery ponds until large enough for stocking. Production of stocking material in ponds may be done by using the simple induced spawning technique, or by the application of pituitary hormone treatment. In both cases, spawning ponds are drained, suitable size pipes are inserted in proper places to serve as spawning nests, and the ponds are refilled with fresh well-oxygenated water before the spawners are introduced. Sexually ripe fish respond quickly to induced spawning treatment; spawning takes place within 24 hours after the injection of the pituitary hormone substance, but within 10 days if they are not injected. Eggs hatch within 20 hours at a water temperature of 28° to 32°C, and start feeding about 4-5 days later when the yolk sacs are completely absorbed.

The Thai catfish stocking rates are the highest found in Southeast Asian fish culture. The range of rate of stocking, size of fingerlings, and duration of culture popularly practiced are shown in Table 9.

TABLE 9.
STOCKING CHARACTERISTICS AND CORRESPONDING CULTURE TIME FOR CATFISH (Thailand)

WEIGHT/FISH STOCKED (grams)	NUMBER OF FISH PER SQUARE METER OF WATER SURFACE	DURATION OF CULTURE (months)
16[A]	80-100	5-6
20	60-80	4-5
25	40-60	3-4

A. Market size: 150-200 grams (1/2 pound).

The presence of such large numbers of fish, combined with poor water circulation, allows the pond to become saturated with organic material. Smelly and black, the water holds very little oxygen, and the pH may fluctuate radically over a 24-hour period. Visitors are often amazed to see fish living under such conditions. There are two reasons catfish can survive in a Thai catfish pond: (1) they are partial air breathers, possessing an accessory respiratory organ above their gill chamber, and (2) they are able to respire through their skin. Nevertheless, catfish farmers drive the fish to the pond surface using mechanical means, such as water flow, to enable them to make use of atmospheric oxygen. If the fish were to rest on the pond bottom, they would die of suffocation. Crowding encourages disease, and disease control and prevention are the most serious problems facing Southeast Asian catfish farmers today. Mortality in some ponds may reach 50%; average mortality by harvest time is 20-30%. At least two crops of fish can be produced per year.

Feed

Catfish culture began in Thailand at the same time that large trawl fisheries were initiated there. Small trash fish unfit for human consumption became plentiful and cheap, and were ideal for use as catfish food. They are the mainstay of the catfish diet; animal offal and scraps from slaughter houses are also sometimes used. Cooked broken rice, rice bran, or aquatic vegetation may be mixed with the animal material to form a ball of food. Feeding is done twice a day, early in the morning and late in the afternoon. The food is thrown into the water by the farmer, who stands on a small plank extending a few feet out over the pond. The farmer stops feeding the fish when feeding activity has slowed down or ceased, usually within 10-15 minutes. Food may also be put into baskets placed at several spots along the edge of the pond. Roughly 6-8% of the body weight of the catfish is fed to them daily. It is difficult to estimate the conversion rate of this fish; approximately 6-8 parts of food produce 1 part fish.

CLARIAS catfish are sold alive in the market. The production cost of 1 kg of Thai catfish is only about $0.44; wholesale price is $0.50/kg, and retail price is about $0.60/kg. This makes the catfish a commodity the ordinary person can afford to buy. Catfish is very popular in Thailand and is usually eaten once or twice a day.

Let us examine the figures showing the estimates of production costs and profits of an average Clarias catfish pond in Thailand (Table 10) more closely. Four thousand kg of fish are harvested every 6 months from 400 square meters of pond. Thus, a 1-hectare catfish pond theoretically should be able to produce 100,000 kg of fish every 6 months, or 750 metric tons per year. A good milkfish pond can produce only 3,000 kg/hectare/year. One must be careful NOT to convert or compare figures in this way. First, a 1-hectare (10,000 m²) pond cannot be managed to grow catfish: 1,000 m² is the largest manageable size. Second, milkfish are raised principally on food grown in the pond itself, while catfish are wholly dependent on introduced feed. When productivity figures (fish produced/unit area of pond) of different types of ponds are compared, they can be very misleading. Many visiting politicians, seeing the astronomical catfish production figures of Thai ponds, and without looking into the details of the operation, have exclaimed, "Oh, this is marvelous, we must introduce this practice to our country." Unfortunately, many such hasty introductions failed. Catfish culture is so successful in Thailand because a plentiful supply of catfish fingerlings is available at little expense from natural habitats where they are easily collected, and abundant trash fish for feed are readily available in the local market year-round.

Nevertheless, Thailand's catfish farmers have run into trouble. Around 1970, when the market demand for catfish was very high and the number of catfish farms was small, produce quickly sold in the market. By 1973 too many ponds were in operation; the market was soon saturated and the ever-increasing surplus production caused fish prices to drop. The cost of production remained the same, and many fish farmers went out of business. So one shouldn't be misled by seemingly high production figures and rush into "lucrative" practices—there is a limit to profitable culture, and that limit is economics.

TABLE 10.

PROJECTED PROFIT AND LOSS STATEMENT PER CROP FOR AN AVERAGE CLARIAS CATFISH POND[A] (Thailand, 1973)

REVENUE	Bahts[B]
Sale of fish (4,000 kg at Bahts 10.0/kg)	40,000
EXPENDITURES	
Interest on capital investment	400
Equipment	500
Maintenance and repair	500
Stocking material (fish)	6,000
Feeds (trash fish, etc.)	26,000
Wages (self-employed = 1/3 person for 6 months)	2,000
TOTAL PRODUCTION EXPENDITURES	35,400
NET INCOME	4,600 or US $230

Source: Ling's estimate
A. An average pond would be 400 square meters in area and 2.5 meters deep. Duration of rearing would be 6 months, and 600 kilograms of Fingerlings would be stocked.
B. 20 Bahts = US $1.

10 Snakehead (*Ophicephalus* spp.) Culture

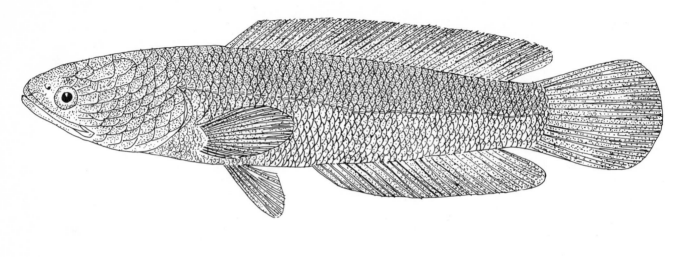

ILLUSTRATION 9.　　　　　Snakehead　　　　*Ophicephalus striatus* Bl. (After Arifin)

The next type of fish culture I would like to discuss is that of the snakehead. This fish has an ugly-looking head like that of a snake, but it possesses abundant firm white flesh, with very few fine bones. Very tasty, it can be prepared in many ways and is a very popular food fish in most Southeast Asian countries. It is extremely hardy and strong, able to survive out of water for long periods of time, and is often believed to have special nutritional value. In Hongkong and Taiwan, snakehead are often consumed by convalescents and elderly people, who believe that it contains some recuperative and strength-generating substance.

The snakehead is also known as *murrel* in India. It is a freshwater fish but able to live in low salinity brackish water. It occurs primarily in shallow areas of lakes, water reservoirs, swamps, marsh pools, flooded lowlands, ponds, ricefields, and other bodies of stagnant or semi-stagnant waters.

The snakehead possesses a suprabranchial cavity in its head, serving as an accessory respiratory organ similar to, but not as well developed as, that of *Clarias* catfish. During the dry season, it is able to settle in the bottom mud of a swamp or ricefield and survive through the period of extremely low water levels. As the process of pond desiccation continues and the bottom dries up, the fish burrows deeper into the moist mud. As long as its skin and breathing organ are kept moist, the snakehead can survive under such conditions for several months without water. After rains it can revive to resume its life activities or to follow small rain-streamlets into newly filled bodies of waters. After a heavy afternoon shower, many snakeheads are often caught by fishermen with hand nets while they are trying to migrate to newly filled waters through shallow rain-streamlets.

The species most commonly cultured is *Ophicephalus striatus*, although other species are also used. It is a carnivorous fish, feeding on aquatic worms, insects, small fish, and other small aquatic animals. It prefers live food, and when it is hungry, it becomes cannibalistic. In tropical waters it is able to attain sexual maturity in about 1 year, but it takes 1.5 to 2 years in temperate waters.

Spawning takes place mostly during the rainy season when there is a plentiful supply of fresh, well-oxygenated water and the water temperature is within the favored range of 26° to 30° C. Mature male and female fish pair off, and together they seek a comparatively well-protected location; here they clear a round-ish area by biting off some of the existing aquatic weeds, and use this as their spawning "nest." Fertilized eggs, owing their buoyancy to the presence of an oil globule, float to the surface, forming a thin film. The male fish stay below or close-by to guard the eggs (and young) against the attacks of enemies such as other fish, frogs, and snakes. Snakehead eggs hatch within three days of incubation. Newly hatched larvae are able to start swimming actively but need to come up to the surface of the water very often to rest and breath. The fry are gregarious and are often seen swimming in a school, churning up and down near the water surface, with the male parent following closely behind to guard and protect them. It takes 6-9 weeks for the fry to lose their gregarious habit and be able to live at the bottom without parental care. They soon assume the habits of adults who come to the surface to take air at long intervals.

Snakehead farming in ponds is a recent development. Before World War II, production from natural sources was so great that, in Thailand alone, there was always a large surplus preserved by sun-drying for export, in addition to the several million pounds consumed by the people annually. Furthermore, because of its car-nivorous food habits, the snakeheads were regarded as dangerous predators and efforts were spent to remove them from ponds instead of culturing them. After World War II, when increased construction of dams and development of hydroelectric operations effectively destroyed many existing snakehead habitats, production of this fish from natural sources decreased rapidly.

Early experiments seeking to increase production of this fish through the development of pond culture were started around 1955 in Thailand and became quite popular in the mid-1960s. Snakehead culture soon spread to the neighboring countries and reached Hong-kong and Taiwan in the early 1970s.

Water Conditions and Pond Preparation

Most of the existing fish ponds can be converted for snakehead culture. For convenience of feeding and management, small ponds ranging from 0.5 to 3 acres are commonly used. Clean fresh water is preferred, and a depth of 4-5 feet is needed. To prevent snakeheads from escaping, the banks of the pond are strengthened and fences are erected at its top. *Ipomoea* (an edible aquatic plant) is often grown in clusters at the corners or along the side of the pond, to provide shade for the fish. The usual practice of pond preparation—drying, leveling, application of insecticides, lime, and fertilizers, refilling with clean water—is followed before stocking.

Stocking Material and Practices

Most stocking material is collected from natural habitats, but some is produced in ponds by artificial propagation. Large numbers of fry and fingerlings can be collected from shallow lakes, swamps, or ricefields with a fine-meshed scoop net during the rainy season. Eggs can be incubated in any kind of basin or tank. Young fry are fed small zooplankton; advanced fry and fingerlings, with chopped worms and minced fish.

Spawning of mature fish can be induced by hypo-physation. The pituitary gland of common carp is homogenized and injected into matured fish. The injected fish are released into a small spawning pond to spawn. Any small fish pond can be used as a spawning pond. The spawning pond may be partitioned into small 3-4 m² compartments with wire or nylon netting material; one pair of fish is introduced into each compartment. An unpartitioned spawning pond can be stocked with several pairs of injected fish. Spawning takes place within 24 hours after the fish have been injected and released.

To minimize chances for cannibalism, single-size stocking is practiced. The rate of stocking varies greatly according to the type of grow-out operation practiced, personal preference, and availability of stocking material and feeds.

Grow-out Operation

The simplest type of snakehead culture makes use of a simple pond left in its natural state. Captured snakehead fingerlings are stocked and allowed to feed on whatever is in the pond or enters later. At the end of the year, 100-200 lbs of fish per acre of water surface area can be obtained from such a simple operation.

Snakehead fingerlings may also be stocked in ponds already being used for culturing other kinds of fish, even in polyculture systems. In most of the fish ponds some small extraneous fish are always present that compete with the cultured fish for food and space. The snakehead is able to control such extraneous pest-fish efficiently and convert them into high-quality fish flesh.

In a polyculture fish pond, the rate of stocking is about 150-200 snakehead fingerlings, 2-3 inches in length, per acre of pond area. Stocking is done when the fish of the polyculture system have already grown to 3-4 inches. Without supplementary feeding, 150-200 lbs of this highly priced snakehead can be harvested from a 1-acre pond annually, in addition to the quantity of fish normally produced.

As market demand for snakehead has increased, experiments to develop more efficient methods for its farming have been conducted. One that has shown promising results is the use of the prolific-breeding, inexpensive tilapia as food for the snakehead. The method may be either simple or elaborate.

A simple operation involves culturing snakehead and tilapia together in the same pond. As soon as the pond is ready to receive fish, sufficient pairs of mature tilapia are introduced first. Snakehead fingerlings are stocked 3-4 weeks later, when the stocked tilapia have already spawned and a large number of tilapia fry have been produced. As long as there is a plentiful supply of tilapia fry as food, very little supplementary feeding is necessary.

A more elaborate operation involves culturing snakehead and tilapia in two separate compartments of the same pond. A 1-hectare pond, for example, is divided into two compartments of unequal size, A and B, by means of a bamboo fence, or nylon netting of suitable mesh size (Fig. 4). Compartment A is about 3,000 m² in size, and Compartment B about 7,000 m², being about 30 percent and 70 percent of the pond area, respectively. Compartment A is for tilapia, Compartment B for snakehead. The entire pond is subjected to the usual preparation procedures. When the preparation operation is completed, Compartment A is heavily fertilized with about 2 tons of farm manure, and Compartment B is provided with clusters of *Ipomoea* plant at its corners and sides. Farm manure serves mostly as fertilizer to promote growth of small organisms that tilapia feed upon, and partly as feed for tilapia directly. *Ipomoea* clusters provide shade for the snakehead. About 2 weeks later, more water is let into the pond to increase the water level to a depth of about 1 meter, and about 2,000 pairs of mature tilapia are introduced into Compartment A. Mature tilapia spawn soon after being stocked and within 2-3 weeks a large quantity of tilapia fry will be produced. At this time, about 3,000 snakehead fingerlings, each weighing about 25 grams, are stocked in Compartment B. Large numbers of tilapia

FIGURE 4.

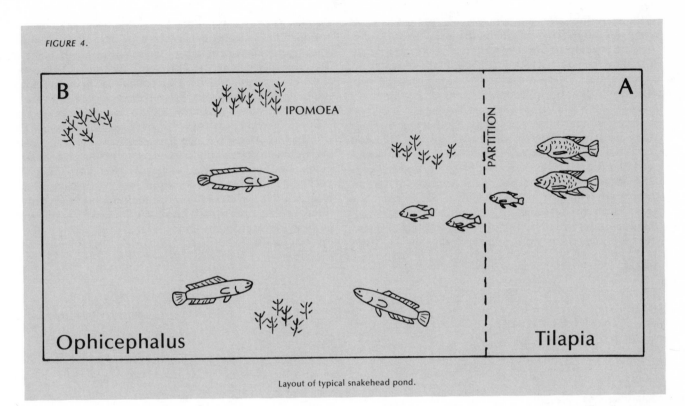

Layout of typical snakehead pond.

fry produced in Compartment A will keep entering Compartment B through the meshed partition, providing food for the snakehead continuously. As the snakehead grow steadily larger, they require more and more food; and when the quantity of tilapia fry that enter into Compartment B from Compartment A is insufficient to meet the demand, supplementary feeding becomes necessary. This is done by catching tilapia fry from Compartment A with hand nets and transferring them to Compartment B, either in early morning or late afternoon, or both. To maintain a high production of tilapia fry, Compartment A is given a supplemental application of about 1 ton of farm manure at monthly intervals during the culturing period.

Given an ample supply of good food and adequate care, snakehead grow fast and survive well in this culture system in tropical waters. At the end of a 10-month culturing period, this 1-hectare pond yields about 2,700 snakehead (90 percent survival of the 3,000 fingerlings stocked), weighing about 2,400 kg (about 800-1,000 grams per fish). This represents a high annual production of about 2,400 kg of snakehead per hectare of pond. Estimates of cost and profits are found in Table 11.

After 8-9 months of culturing, some of the fish may have already grown to marketable size, and, if so desired, partial harvesting may be done with either cast-net or seine-net, to capture some of the large specimens for the market. Complete harvesting is done at the end of the culturing period, by draining the pond and capturing the fish by hand or with hand nets.

The snakehead are transported alive to the market in shallow containers with a small amount of water or in wet gunny sacks, and are always sold alive. Dead snakehead have very little market value.

In such a culture system, the greatest expenses are fertilizer for the tilapia and snakehead fingerlings for stocking material. Snakehead fingerlings are obtained from special hatcheries or from the wild and cost about NT $10 (US $.25) each. Snakehead culture can be profitable because snakeheads fetch a high price; in Taiwan people are willing to pay NT $100 (US $2.50) per kilogram. Formerly in Hongkong, Taiwan, and areas where the fish was scarce and the price high, substantial quantities of snakehead were imported alive by air from Cambodia or Thailand. Recently, (1975) because of over-production, snakehead farmers were having the same kind of economic problem as catfish farmers in Thailand. The pioneers made a lot of money. Those who entered the industry later obtained successful fish harvests but failed to make a profit. The market is flooded, and selling prices have gone down while the cost of production has remained the same or even increased because of inflation. A new balance between cost of production and profit must be struck in order to make snakehead culture monetarily rewarding again. This is one of the overriding problems in development of fish culture in Asia and the Far East. The old traditional methods produced a small but steady profit for generations of fish farmers. New techniques bring sizable profits only in the first few years.

TABLE 11.

PROJECTED ANNUAL PROFIT AND LOSS STATEMENT FOR AN AVERAGE SNAKEHEAD POND[A] (TAIWAN, 1973)

REVENUE	NT (New Taiwan dollar)[B]
Sale of fish (2400 kg at NT $80/kg)	$192,000
EXPENDITURES	
Interest on capital investment	NT $ 10,000
Equipment	5,000
Maintenance and repair	4,000
Stocking material (fingerlings)	30,000
Tilapia (primarily for forage)	15,000
Feed and fertilizer	30,000
Wages (1/2 person)	18,000
Miscellaneous	3,000
TOTAL PRODUCTION EXPENDITURES	$115,000
NET INCOME	NT $ 77,000 or US $1,925

Source: Ling's estimate.

A. Pond would be 1 hectare (2.47 acres) in area and 1 meter deep. Stocked would be 3,000 snakehead fingerlings (about 15 centimeters in length and 25 grams in weight) and 600 kilograms or about 2,000 pairs of tilapia (primarily for forage). The fish would be cultured for 10 months, and the expected mortality rate would be about 10 percent.

B. New Taiwan dollar (NT $40 = US $1).

11 Freshwater Eel (Anguilla japonica) Culture

Several species of freshwater eel are cultured in Southeast Asia, but the most popular is *Anguilla japonica*. This species occurs naturally in Japan, Korea, China, and several other countries in the area, where many claim that its taste is distinguishably superior to that of other anguillids. In Japan this eel is one of the most expensive fish in the market; one pound of whole eel costs about $15.

We still do not know much about the life history of this eel, but it is probably very similar to that of the European species, *Anguilla anguilla*. As far as we know, the eels enter freshwater rivers, lakes, or streams as elvers and spend from 3-4 years there until they become adults (1-1.5 pounds). They then leave their home waters to enter the sea. As the eels migrate out to sea, their gonads steadily develop until they reach full maturity. It is suspected that the eels' spawning ground is a deep spot in the sea southwest of Taiwan. After spawning, the eels die, never to return. The leaflike leptocephalus larvae migrate back to the coastal areas as plankton. Carried by currents, they slowly develop into transparent glass eels or elvers. As the elvers enter fresh water at the entrance to rivers they are caught in hand nets by eel farmers for stocking purposes.

Attempts to breed *A. japonica* artificially have not yet been successful. Although eels have been kept in ponds for 3-4 years, mature specimens have never been obtained. In Japan and Taiwan experimentation with pituitary hormone (or HCG) treatment has been initiated. Full-grown male and female eels are injected with small amounts of the hormones at regular intervals. After several months, the gonads show definite signs of development; on several occasions the females' ovaries have actually grown to full size, some containing well-formed, mature eggs. In a few cases the testes of male eels have fully matured also. Complete success in artificial fertilization will probably come in a few years.

Farming of *A. japonica* is done on a large scale only in Japan and Taiwan, but pilot-scale experimental farming is being conducted in many Southeast Asian countries. Eel culture began in Japan 50 years ago but shows its most phenomenal development in Taiwan. Before 1952 all eels were caught cheaply in rivers and lakes and used as duck feed or fish bait. In 1952 a pilot-scale experimental eel farm was established. After successful results had repeatedly been obtained and reported, the first few small commercial eel farms were established in 1966. At that time the total acreage of eel ponds was only 66 hectares belonging to about 10 companies. During the following 8 years, there was a meteoric increase in eel pond acreage (see Table 12).

TABLE 12.
TOTAL AREA OF COMMERCIAL EEL FARMS FOR SELECTED YEARS (TAIWAN, AFTER 1952)

YEAR	HECTARES[A]	YEAR	HECTARES[A]
1952	[B]	1971	660
1966	66	1972	1,058
1967	80	1973	1,200

A. 1 hectare = 2.47 acres.
B. No commercial eel farms—a few experimental ponds only.

The greatest increase in eel farms occurred from 1969 through 1972, coinciding with a sudden surge in demand for eels in Japan. At this time the Japanese were enjoying the benefits of an economic boom; many Japanese companies had lavish expense accounts for public relations entertaining. Japanese were willing to pay exorbitant prices for eels, and although prices skyrocketed, many could now afford to buy them. As the demand for eel jumped sky high, the local Japanese market could not satisfy it and so began importing eels from Taiwan. Ready markets and high profits are strong inducements. Eel farmers already in the business increased existing acreage, other fish farmers converted their ponds to eel culture, and investors were attracted to establish new farms. Then came the economic crisis of 1973. Demand for eel rapidly diminished; there was suddenly no market for the increased harvest of eels. With keen competition for the Tokyo market not only between Taiwan farmers, but with Japanese eel farmers, the market price dropped from $15 to $4-$5 a pound. Many eel farmers went bankrupt, and the increase in eel pond acreage has slowed down considerably.

Stocking

Before the establishment of commercial eel farms in Taiwan in 1966, elvers had no real market value. When eel culture began to boom, the demand for glass eels as stocking material skyrocketed, as did their market value. There were not enough elvers collected in Japan to satisfy the Japanese farmers, and so elvers were imported from Taiwan. Table 13 showing the cost of elvers in Taiwan reflects the fantastic growth of eel farming. Competition forced prices up daily until very few eel farmers could afford to buy enough elvers to stock their ponds.

TABLE 13.

COST OF ELVERS (TAIWAN, AFTER 1952)

YEAR	COST PER KILOGRAM (US DOLLARS)
1952	$ 0.25
1966	1.50A
1970	150.00B
1973	1,000.00C

A. Beginning of commercial eel farming.
B. Rapid expansion of eel farms.
C. Height of expansion of eel farming.

At the height of the demand for young *Anguilla japonica* ($1,000/kg), *A. anguilla* glass eels could be obtained from Europe for only $50-$100/kg, including trans-portation. Nevertheless, local farmers did not want this foreign species; they felt the European elvers might be susceptible to local diseases, might grow poorly, and might lack consumer appeal. Since it is extremely difficult to distinguish European eel (*A. anguilla*) elvers from *A. japonica* elvers, importers smuggled them in illegally. Some of the smuggled shipments were even sent in covered wagons to coastal areas where local collectors were netting native glass eels. There they were put into hired boats whose crew would row out, pretend to fish, and come back to shore to sell the imported elvers as local produce. The eel farmers waiting patiently on the shore were sure these elvers were 100% "genuine." They realized their mistake only after several weeks of culturing. The European elvers grew slowly, were prone to catch local diseases, could not adapt well to foreign water conditions, and frequently suffered high mortalities. After many such difficulties, eel farmers eventually attempted to incorporate new methods of culture, using new species of eels, with traditional *A. japonica* culture. Species that are now being experimented with include: (1) *Anguilla rostrata* (native to the U.S.); (2) *A. pacificus* (from Indonesia and the Philippines); (3) *A. bicolor* (from Indonesia and the Philippines); (4) *A. pacificus* (from Australia and New Zealand); (5) *A. anguilla* (from Europe). Although these eels command a lower price on the market, the price of their elvers is correspondingly lower.

There are two stages involved in the culture of eels: raising the glass eels to stocking size, and raising the young stocked eels to market size in ponds. Glass eels are reared in small cement troughs, tanks, or shallow cement ponds. These are supplied with fresh, well-oxygenated, running water and are covered to protect them from direct sunlight, rainfall, or sudden temperature fluctuation. The tanks and ponds can be disinfected before use, and the farmers have good control over water quality and temperature. When wild glass eels are first put into the tanks, they refuse to feed, and must be trained to take artificial feeds. A small tray is filled with a ground paste of aquatic earthworms, clams, oysters, and fresh fish meat, and is then lowered into the bottom of the tank at night. After one or two days the boldest eels approach the food; within 20 days all the glass eels are feeding from the tray. Gradually the position of the feeding tray is raised from the tank bottom to just under the water surface while the feeding time is changed from night to morning. This usually takes from 2 weeks to 1 month. Expensive items in the feed, such as oysters, clams, and earthworms, are then gradually replaced with minced trash fish while the feeding tray is exchanged for a wire mesh basket. On some farms, small amounts of formulated high protein food composed of fish meal, soybean, corn, minerals, and vitamins are mixed with the feed to which the elvers are accustomed, and gradually used to replace it. Young eels may be kept in the nursery ponds or tanks for 4-5 months; they are subsequently transferred to the grow-out ponds.

Ponds

Eels are grown to market size in freshwater ponds ranging in size from 0.1 to 0.5 hectare. Large companies occasionally have ponds as large as 1.5 hectares, although this is a little too big for convenient operation. When fast-running water is used, smaller ponds with stronger walls are constructed and stocking can be much higher in these ponds. Ponds with sluggish water flow are usually on the large side. All ponds are shallow; only a small amount of mud is removed to build the bunds. Not only are deep ponds difficult to drain, but they are too expensive to excavate. The earthen bunds of an eel pond are reinforced with a layer of brick to prevent the eels from boring holes through them and escaping.

Eels are quite sensitive to low levels of dissolved oxygen and to water pollution. Mechanical means are often used to increase aeration, especially during the summer or at night when the danger of rapid oxygen depletion is high. Water wheels operated by foot or run by electric generators, water agitators, water sprayers, or airstones may be used. Water pollution is an ever-increasing danger, especially in agricultural areas where pesticides and insecticides are being used more frequently. Whenever possible, underground water from artesian wells is used to supply the ponds. Since this water contains very little oxygen, it is pumped into a reservoir tank and agitated vigorously before being passed down through pipes into the pond.

In Taiwan it is necessary to have a source of underground water that can be fed into the pond in winter to maintain a suitable water temperature for the eels. Water in a standing pond in winter will drop to 10°C; at this temperature the eels become sluggish and cease feeding. The geothermal heat supplied by artesian well water will maintain the pond temperature at 20°C. Although this is still not the optimum temperature for eel growth, it will alleviate their susceptibility to illness and allow them to feed.

Feed

In eel grow-out ponds, trash fish are primarily used as feed. The trash fish are either parboiled whole or ground raw into a pulp (sometimes mixed with soybean, corn, rice bran, or other material), and then placed in wire-mesh feeding baskets. The baskets are lowered into the pond at the same time every day from a feeding platform. This platform is built 10-12 feet out over the water from the bund. Various numbers of baskets are used, depending on the number of eels in the pond. Most of the eels begin to congregate at the feeding platform shortly before the feeder arrives. As soon as a basket is lowered, thousands of eels, fighting like a wild, live ball of entangled rope, burrow into the food mass, eating greedily. Within 5-10 minutes most of them depart, leaving fish skeletons without a trace of flesh. The basket is either removed when all the eels have left, or after 20 minutes (found by experience to be sufficient time for all eels to feed). It is estimated that the eels consume 5-10% of their body weight in feed daily. The conversion rate using trash fish as feed is claimed to be 8 or 10:1.

Invariably with this type of feeding, a large amount of material drops to the bottom of the pond to decay. The resulting nutrients may stimulate the growth of any number of small organisms. Rather than draining the pond and refilling it with fresh water, the fish farmer first roughly estimates the nature and quantity of organisms polluting the pond or potentially unhealthy for the eels. If the pond is swarming with zooplankton, bighead carp are stocked. Silver carp are added to ponds suffering from phytoplankton blooms and common carp are used to control benthic algae, insects, and worms. At harvest time the eel farmer can usually obtain at least 100 kilograms of fish/hectare/annum in addition to eels. The pollution problem is solved simply, without the aid of chemicals, and a profit may even be made.

Young eels do not grow at the same rate. After several months a disparity in size is evident, and it becomes more marked as the smaller eels compete less effectively with the larger ones for food. To avoid the eels' cannibalistic tendencies and to encourage the growth of the smaller ones, the eels are periodically sorted by size and cultured in separate ponds.

Harvesting

Eel harvesting may be selective or total. Selective harvesting is usually first done 6 months after the initial stocking and every week from then on. A large pocket net is laid below the feeding platform at night. In the morning food is placed in the usual area. While the eels are busily engaged in feeding, the net is closed from the top. Captured eels are segregated by size; small ones are released into separate grow-out ponds while large ones are taken for the market. A good season for eel harvesting is August-September-October, when there is a great demand for eels in Japan and Taiwan. At the end of the year in Taiwan, before the cold winter sets in, there is a complete, or total harvest. The entire pond is drained and all the eels are collected. Those too small for the market are kept in the wintering pond and re-released for further culture the next year. Market-size

eels in Japan range from 150-200 grams each. The Taiwan and Hongkong consumers prefer larger eels weighing from 250-300 grams apiece. Table 14 shows projected profits for a 1-hectare eel farm.

Transportation to Market

Every effort is made to sell the eels alive, for as soon as they die their market value decreases to about one-fourth the live value. Since there is usually some distance between the pond and market, the following simple method is used to keep the eels alive for the journey. The eels are first collected and placed in a running water trough or cement conditioning-pond to void their wastes. They are then cornered into a small area of the trough or transferred to a small container where the water temperature is gradually lowered from 20°C to 10-15°C by the addition of ice. At this temperature the eels become sluggish, require less oxygen, and are less susceptible to injury. For transportation to the market,

TABLE 14.

PROJECTED ANNUAL PROFIT AND LOSS STATEMENT FOR A 1-HECTARE EEL FARM (Taiwan, 1973)

REVENUE	NT (New Taiwan dollar)A	
Sale of eels (650 kg at NT $150/kg)		$97,500
EXPENDITURES		
Interest on capital investment	NT $ 2,000	
Equipment	2,000	
Maintenance and repair	1,000	
Stocking material (small eel)	45,000	
Feed	20,000	
Water and power	1,500	
Wages (1/4 person)	10,000	
Miscellaneous	1,000	
TOTAL PRODUCTION EXPENDITURES		$82,500
NET INCOME	NT $15,000 = US $375	

Source: Ling's estimate
A. New Taiwan dollar (NT $40 = U.S. $1).

the chilled eels are placed in shallow, waterproof baskets lined with moss or moist sawdust to prevent desiccation. On top of these baskets are placed other baskets filled with ice; as the ice melts it slowly drips down onto the eels, keeping them moist and chilled.

For transportation to Japan, the chilled, conditioned eels are placed in plastic bags containing a little water and small packages of dry ice. The bags are inflated with oxygen and packed in strong cartons or boxes insulated with plastic foam. The boxes are shipped by air to Tokyo, where the eels are revived by slow raising of water temperature. The survival rate of eels shipped in this manner is usually 90-95%, and sometimes as high as 99%.

12 Pen Culture

"Pen culture" is not a well-defined term. Pens first referred to temporary salt pans (natural depressions in the earth) on the coastal flats in Asia, used part of the year as fish ponds. During the 6 months of dry season, sea water enters these areas and evaporates to form crystallized rock salt. During the rainy season, the pans are diluted by fresh rain water. People heighten the bunds and trap fish and shrimp within the resulting enclosures. Many of the original salt pans are now being converted for permanent use in fish and shrimp culture. These facilities, not as elaborate as ponds, are known as pens, and culture within them is known as pen culture.

Shallow areas along the edges of lakes or reservoirs are sometimes dammed, and a constant water level is maintained within the enclosure by pumps. When these areas are used to culture fish, they are included in the loose term of pen culture.

The "corral" type of fish culture practiced in the Philippines is also included under pen culture. Bamboo poles, sticks, twigs, and similar material are used to make the frames of corrals. They are planted a few feet apart in the bottom of the shallow areas of a lake (2-3 meters deep) in the form of a circle or square. Nylon or wire netting is fastened to the poles to form an enclosed area. Corrals are built high enough above the surface of the water to prevent the fish from escaping during heavy rains.

The corral type of fish culture has proven to be extremely suitable in areas where the water is naturally rich in food substances. A good example is Lake Lagona in Manila, the Philippines. This shallow, lakelike lagoon collects water from a vast area of land, hills, and streams.

The drainage system of the lagoon is poor because of its small outlet to the sea. This, combined with the heavy daily input of sewage from hundreds of families living in the surrounding villages and cities, makes the lake extremely rich in organic material. Before the introduction of corral fish culture, the lake was so full of phytoplankton that it was actually as green and thick as pea soup. Millions and millions of midge larvae thrived on the rich sludge at the bottom of the lake. Periodically they emerged in enormous numbers like a huge black cloud, clogging ventilators, pipes, windshields, and homes. The people complained, the politicians made noise, and the fisheries experts were blamed. For years these scientists tried to destroy the midges with various expensive chemicals. In one or two weeks some of the midges would be exterminated and celebrations would begin. Before the celebrations were over, however, the midges would arise again. They became a dominant political issue of the day, as was the general condition of the lake.

Eventually it was decided to use fish to help solve the problem. The phytoplankton bloom in the lake consisted of a type of algae very few fish could digest. Milkfish were experimentally stocked in corrals constructed inside the lake. The young milkfish grew even faster in the corrals than those cultured in ponds, where an elaborate series of technical operations must be performed to promote the growth of benthic algae (See Chapter 8 on milkfish culture). The milkfish greedily consumed the rich phytoplankton crop in the lake. Since enriched water is continuously being fed into the lake, there is a virtually unlimited food supply for the milkfish. When cultured in a well-constructed corral in Lake Lagona, young milkfish fingerlings can grow to market size in 4 rather than 6 months. Area for area, the corrals can produce more milkfish/hectare/year than a milkfish pond. There are now hundreds of corrals in Lake Lagona. Not only are they a profitable business enterprise, but they help control excessive algal blooms and troublesome midges.

This is a point that should be stressed. Presently there are eutrophication problems in many United States lakes and waters. People complain, various chemicals (many with unknown and potentially devastating effects) are used, and much money is spent; but the problems keep recurring. The stocking of planktiverous fish should be tried as a partial solution. Exotic species might cause complications, but native phytoplankton feeders should be satisfactory. Even if these fish cannot be used for human consumption, control of phytoplankton blooms is reward enough for their stocking.

13 Cage Culture

Cage culture in Southeast Asia has a long history. We believe that it began with fishermen who tried to keep their surplus catch alive for the market. Extra fish were put into small baskets hanging in the water alongside their boats or floating houses. The fishermen's wives threw kitchen garbage into the baskets and in many cases the fish grew markedly. Gradually the temporary surplus baskets were modified into culturing cages and developed into a very efficient, productive type of aquaculture.

Three countries in Southeast Asia—Indonesia, Cambodia, and Thailand—are each noted for their own unique form of cage culture. Cages are made of wood, bamboo, or rattan. Their dimensions are usually 2 x 3 x 0.5 meters, although they range from a small size of 1 x 2 x 1 meter to large sizes of 3 to 5 meters x 5 to 16 meters x 1.5 to 3 meters. Large cages are usually partitioned into several compartments. One family usually manages a group of two to six cages, tied together as a unit.

In Indonesia alone, cages are set directly on the bottom of streams and are anchored there with large stones to keep them from being washed away, especially during heavy winter storms. Only a few streams are suitable for this type of cage culture. These streams pass through large farming villages where sewage consisting of animal and human waste empties into them. As this organic material is carried downstream, it breaks down into nutrients that support rich benthic populations of midges, insect larvae, aquatic worms, copepods, and rotifers. The Indonesians set their fish cages far enough downstream to allow adequate degradation of the sewage while still allowing the enclosed fish to benefit from the enriched sources of fish food. Slits in the cages allow water laden with small living organisms to flow through into the fishes' mouths. Only common carp *(Cyprinus carpio)* are stocked in Indonesian fish cages.

The stocking rate is proportional to the area of the cage bottom; for every square meter of bottom, 100 fish weighing 20-30 grams each are stocked. In an average cage (2 x 3 x 1.5 meters), 600 young carp would be stocked. Within 6-8 months, these fish will each grow to 400-600 grams with no supplemental feeding. In 10-12 months' time, they can reach 800-1,000 grams. If we initially stock 600 fish in a cage (12 kg total) and allow a standard 20% mortality rate, we will obtain about 480 kilograms of fish at the end of one year. This production rate of about 80 kg of carp/square meter/year does not involve much care or expense. If there is not enough food naturally present in the water, either the density of stocked fish is reduced or supplemental feed is added to the cages. During bad weather (heavy rains or severe flood), supplemental feed may also be given. Supplemental feeds consist of a number of materials such as cooked broken rice, rice bran, ground dried trash fish, or peanut cake. Culture cages are constructed with doors on the top, and the fish farmer can easily harvest the size and number of fish he desires at any time.

Another type of cage culture is practiced in Cambodia (Khmer). Cambodian cages are usually 3 x 4 x 2 meters in size. Large cages are made of wood, smaller ones of bamboo or rattan. They are stocked with either the *Pangasius* catfish, *Ophicephalus* (snakehead), or *Clarias* catfish, in that order of importance. Cage culture using other species of fish has recently been experimented with, but the first three remain the most important fish in Cambodian cage culture.

Cages are set in great densities along the banks of mildly flowing rivers. The most popular area lies along the sides of the tributary joining the Mekong River to Cambodia's vast inland lake. Unlike cages in Indonesia, Cambodian cages are suspended in the water with the upper edges about ½ meter above the water surface and the bottoms about ½ meter above the river bed. They are supported by floats or tied to poles or floating houses. Natural flow of water through the cage provides aeration for the fish. Three years ago, before the present political unrest, there were about 1,000 cages in operation in Cambodia. Some were set individually, others in groups covering large areas of water. Every year these cages produced a total of approximately 3,000 tons of fish; each cage, on the average, produced 3 tons of fish a year.

The stocking rate in Cambodian cage culture is very high, higher than that used in Indonesian cage culture. All of the young fish used for stocking are collected from their natural habitats; there are still no hatcheries in Cambodia that can produce *Pangasius* fingerlings.

The rivers in which Cambodian cages are set carry small quantities of natural food, and Cambodian cage culture relies entirely on heavy supplemental feeding. Large quantities of trash fish are obtained from the inland lake during the rainy season. At this time the lake, acting as a reservoir, fills with water and fish populations within increase rapidly. As water begins to drain from the lake into the Mekong River, Cambodian fishermen set nets and V-traps within the many small emptying

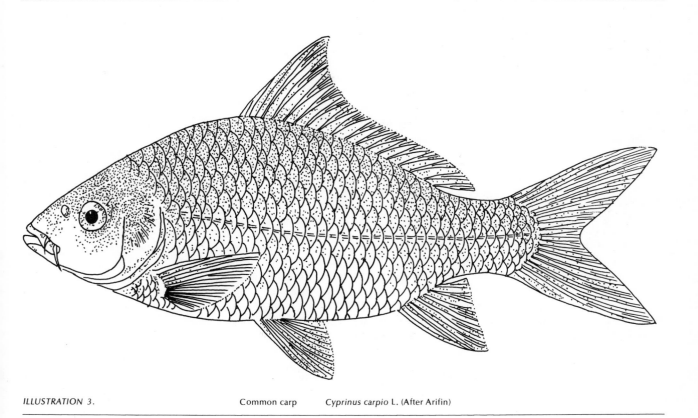

ILLUSTRATION 3.   Common carp   *Cyprinus carpio* L. (After Arifin)

tributaries. For four months of every year, an abundant supply of fish is caught in this way. Large fish are marketed for human consumption while small ones are used as feed in cage culture. During this period of abundance, the *Pangasius* are fed 10-15% of their body weight 2 to 3 times a day and they grow rapidly. During the dry season, trash fish cannot be easily obtained, and fish farmers must use leftover dried fish or purchase fish meal and mix it with a large amount of corn, potato wastes, rice bran, aquatic vegetation, or any kitchen wastes to serve as feed. Feeding is severely reduced, and the fish, barely able to sustain themselves, grow extremely slowly. It takes 8-10 pounds of trash fish to grow 1 pound of *Pangasius* catfish in Cambodian cage culture.

In a typical Cambodian cage (3 x 4 x 2 meters), 6,000 fingerlings weighing 40 grams apiece would be stocked (see Table 15). Allowing for as much as 50%

TABLE 15.
STOCKING RATES FOR CAGE CULTURED PANGASIUS (Cambodia)

NUMBER FISH STOCKED PER CAGE	AVERAGE WEIGHT OF EACH FISH (grams)	TOTAL WEIGHT STOCKED (kilograms)
500	40	20
300	100	30
200	200	40

mortality during the growing period, the harvest should be 3,000 fish, each weighing 1 kilogram or more, at the end of the year. Thus each cage can produce about 3,000 kg of fish/year.

Although the caged catfish production figures are impressive, there are many problems involved in this kind of culture: (1) There are not as many young fish as desired for stocking material. (2) Disease is frequently a problem because of the high densities of fish stocked in the cages. (3) In the dry season when feed is quite expensive, a poor farmer often must sell his cage. (4) Poor workmanship often allows holes or weak spots to develop in the cages. Fish farmers have developed a very simple method of detecting holes before many of the cultured *Pangasius* can escape. Into each cage they place a known number (usually about 10) of *Clarias* catfish as indicators. The *Clarias* catfish are very dark and quite distinct from the pale *Pangasius* catfish. Because they are very greedy and wily, they are usually the first to come for food and the first to escape if any breakage should occur. At feeding time the farmers count the number of *Clarias* present. If any are missing, the hole can usually be found and repaired before many of the *Pangasius* escape. There are no good indicator species used in *Clarias* catfish or snakehead cage culture.

Cage culture in Thailand is basically the same as that in Cambodia. Although the methods of culture and the fish used are the same in both countries, stocking and feeding rates are much lower in Thailand, where trash fish (for feed) are not as plentiful. In Thailand, induced breeding of the *Pangasius* has already been accomplished by hormone treatment, and fingerlings are produced in hatcheries for stocking. While Cambodian cages are placed in rivers away from the farmers' homes, cages in Thailand are tied to the farmers' floating houses along the sides of rivers. This could be due to tradition. In Cambodia cage farmers have a strong union and poaching is strictly controlled. In Thailand poachers are a real problem. Cages must be kept close to home where they can be watched constantly.

In addition to the traditional forms of cage culture, there is the so-called "net-cage" culture popularly used in Japan to culture porgy, groupers, and yellowtail. Net cage culture has been introduced into Southeast Asia on an experimental basis. However, in coastal areas the nets soon become clogged with algae, and at least one standby net must always be on hand. The high cost of these nets and the fouling problems involved seem prohibitive to rapid development of this form of culture.

14 Ricefield Fish Culture

Rice is the staple food of the people of Southeast Asia; most of their agricultural production consists of rice. Villagers are all acquainted with ricefield management and pay close attention to preparing and fertilizing the ricefields. The resulting rich supply of plant nutrients promotes luxurious growth of weeds and algae among the rice plants. These support a large population of crustaceans, worms, and insect larvae, which make wonderful fish food. From the time ricefields are prepared for planting of rice seedlings, many small fish enter them naturally through irrigation canals. In the 4-5 inches of water present in the field, the fish grow readily and can be caught by the farmers at the end of the rice-growing season. Progressive farmers gradually improved the natural fish stocking and growing processes, developing a system of aquaculture known as ricefield-fish (paddy-cum-fish) culture. Paddy-cum-fish farming may be divided into three categories: fish grown in the field at the same time rice is, fish grown alternately with rice crops, and the total conversion of ricefields into fish ponds.

Growing of rice and fish at the same time has shown great promise. Not only can valuable protein be obtained at very little additional cost to the farmer, but rice production can be boosted as much as 5%. Successful paddy-cum-fish farming of this type hinges on the proper selection of suitable fish and rice varieties. Both fish and rice must be able to withstand a great deal of fluctuation in water level. The rice plants should have strong root systems. Fish should grow rapidly, preferably reaching market size within the 3-4 month rice-growing period. They should not consume any part of the rice plants. There are many advantages to growing rice and fish in a field at the same time: (1) Fish consuming harmful insect larvae and worms aid in controlling these rice-paddy pests. (2) Fish feeding on algae and aquatic weeds reduce competition with the rice plants for nutrition and space. (3) In searching for food the fish disturb the bottom of the field, introducing oxygen into the soil layers and increasing the rate of mineralization. (4) Fecal matter of the fish serves as useful fertilizer.

Different fish are used in different countries to stock ricefields. Common carp are stocked successfully in ricefields throughout Southeast Asia. In Malaysia and Thailand, the Siamese gourami is used. This fish grows rapidly, reaching market size within the 3-4 months of the rice-growing season, and it can be harvested just prior to the rice harvest. Young Siamese gouramies often enter the ricefields naturally through irrigation canals. This process can be improved with human assistance. In Malaysia large numbers of mature Siamese gouramies are stocked in suitable locations in irrigation ditches. Here they propagate rapidly, producing large numbers of offspring, which find their way (or are driven) through the feeder canals into the ricefields. The annual production of fish can be increased up to 50% when this method is used.

Indonesia has the most extensive and progressive paddy-cum-fish culture in Southeast Asia. A great deal of controlled stocking is performed there. Indonesians are accustomed to eating the small fish (3-4 inches) that can be grown so readily in ricefields. These fish are gutted, fried, and eaten whole. Common carp, *Puntius* carp, and tilapia are stocked in high densities, varying with the fertility of the ricefield. If the fish must still be grown after the short rice-growing period has ended, the paddy field is specially prepared. Ditches about 2-3 feet deep are dug along the sides of the field; a slightly deeper pit is constructed at the end of the field where water drainage takes place. When the rice is harvested, water is drained from the field, and the fish are driven into the ditches and pit. They are kept here until the field has been prepared for the next rice planting and water has been reintroduced. The fish can then be released back into the field to grow for a second season. The side ditches and pit are also useful for holding fish when pesticides are being applied to the rice. Rice is susceptible to many kinds of insects and disease, and with the introduction of modern farming techniques, more and more chemical pesticides are being used. Many of these chemicals are poisonous to fish. To reduce the hazards of chemical exposure to the fish, the field is drained and the fish are driven into the side ditches before the pesticides are applied. Unfortunately, this is not always effective. In recent years paddy-cum-fish culture has been drastically reduced in those countries where pesticides are used intensively. Research is now being conducted to find pesticides harmless to fish; until this is done, synchronous rice-fish culture appears doomed to suffer slow progress or even decline.

The second category of fish-cum-paddy culture includes ricefields in which fish are grown alternately with rice. Fish may be cultured in the ricefields during the

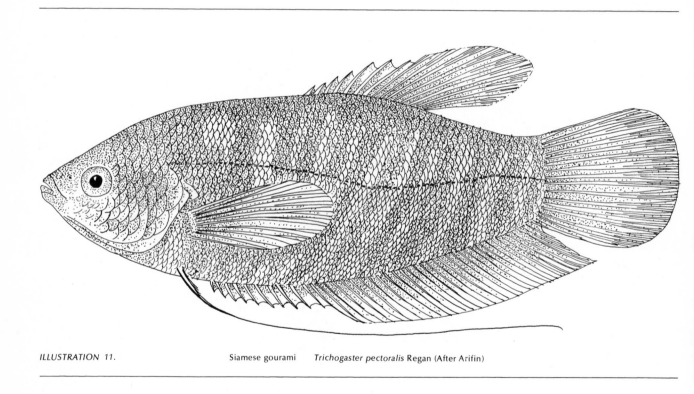

ILLUSTRATION 11.   Siamese gourami   *Trichogaster pectoralis* Regan (After Arifin)

traditional 3-4 month rest period between the two annual rice-growing seasons, or fish and rice farming may be alternated in any combination of desired intervals. In this type of culture the fish are not directly exposed to the dangers of pesticides. Kinds and size of fish to be stocked and rates of stocking are controlled in all cases by the farmer.

Lastly, if rice production in a field proves uneconomical, the field may be converted temporarily or permanently to fish culture. In Thailand many low-production paddyfields have been converted to the culture of Siamese gourami, *Clarias* catfish. etc. In Hongkong, several hundred acres of poor ricefield have been converted into highly productive fish ponds. In Taiwan, the acreage of low production ricefields converted to polyculture of fish or fish-cum-duck culture has increased so much and so rapidly in some districts that further conversion is now being regulated by the government.

15 Polyculture

The success of freshwater aquaculture in Southeast Asia is due principally to the application of polyculture techniques. The culture of a single species of fish alone (monoculture) can be profitable, but the best, most efficient kind of production is obtained through polyculture.

Polyculture involves raising several different compatible fish species and sometimes other economic aquatic organisms together. They need complementary life and feeding habits that enable them to live harmoniously in all the accessible ecological niches and to make optimum use of, and remain in balance with, all types and quantities of food material available in the culturing pond.

Any given body of water supports an abundance of life, linked through a complex food chain usually beginning with simple plants like microscopic phytoplankton and terminating with carnivorous fish. There will be continuous fluctuation in the components of the food chain, but over the long period a balance is maintained. Pond organisms can be classified in a number of ways: according to whether they are found in the bottom, middle, or surface layers of water; according to their mobility; and according to whether they are plants or animals. Plants and animals living on the pond bottom are termed the "benthos." This usually includes algae, diatoms, worms, insects, molluscs, benthic copepods, microscopic bacteria, and fungi. Organisms drifting in the water, carried by currents, are called plankton. Plankton containing chlorophyll is known as phytoplankton; animal plankton, or zooplankton, is made up primarily of small crustaceans. Animals able to move of their own accord through the water column (insect larvae, small shrimps, fish) are collectively called "nekton." Large algae and higher plants, usually attached to the bottom, are termed "macrophytes." These artificial categories are used for the sake of convenience in the following discussion.

The basic objective of polyculture is to raise a proper number of mixed species of fish that are best able to convert all the types of food material a pond can produce into their protein as cheaply and efficiently as possible. Rough calculations are first made of: (1) the quantity and quality of each type of potential food available in the pond; (2) the extent to which production of each of these groups can be increased (e.g. by better water quality management or the application of fertilizers); and (3) their rates of growth and replenishment. From this information, the species, size, and numbers of fish to be stocked and the times of stocking are determined.

Figure 5 illustrates some of the relationships between the major groups of food organisms present in a Southeast Asian polyculture pond and the types of fish stocked to utilize them. Pyramid A displays the principal groups of organisms found in a polyculture pond. The area assigned to each category corresponds roughly to its percentage of the total pond biota by weight. For example, phytoplankton and microzooplankton make up the bulk of the pond biota in a well-fertilized pond. Pyramid B displays fish commonly stocked in Southeast Asian ponds to utilize adjacent organisms in Pyramid A. In the area corresponding to phytoplankton, silver carp, a very efficient phytoplankton feeder, is listed. The grey mullet and bighead carp feed on both phytoplankton and zooplankton; therefore a dotted line is used to demarcate them from the silver carp, which may also consume zooplankton. The grass carp eats macrophytes as efficiently as a cow eats grass. Common carp, mud carp, and black carp are stocked to utilize the benthos. Carnivorous species, such as perch, able to fit into a polyculture system harmoniously, may be stocked in the pond to utilize the nekton. However, young carnivorous fish are never introduced into a polyculture pond until the other cultured fish are large or swift enough to escape predation. The fish listed in this diagram have been used in Chinese polyculture systems for a long time. In Southeast Asia, either these or native fish with similar food habits are stocked. Grass carp can be interchanged with the *Puntius* carp or giant gourami. Organisms other than fish, such as freshwater prawns (*Macrobrachium* spp.) may also be stocked in polyculture ponds, and marine shrimps and crabs may be stocked with milkfish. In coastal areas, clams and mussels are sometimes used in place of, or to supplement, silver carp as phyto-plankton feeders. Some seaweed and aquatic vegetations have also been cultivated in polyculture fish ponds.

Stocking Material

Stocking material of the various species of fish (mainly major carps) popularly used in a polyculture system is obtained either from natural habitats or from

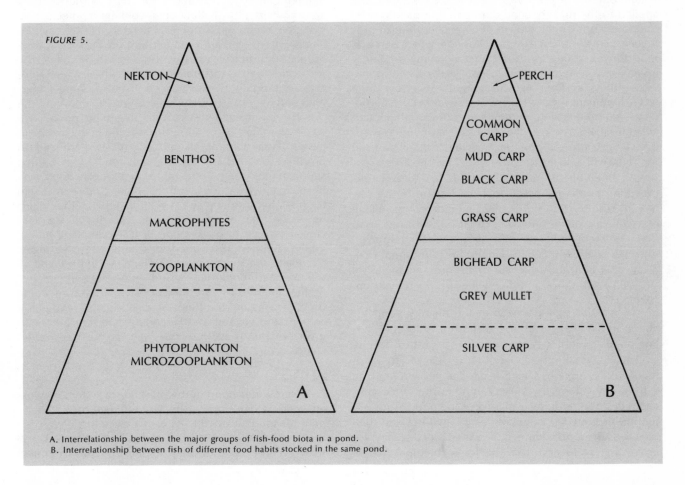

FIGURE 5.

A. Interrelationship between the major groups of fish-food biota in a pond.
B. Interrelationship between fish of different food habits stocked in the same pond.

hatcheries as discussed previously. Young fry that have newly developed mouths and that are just passing the yolk-sac stage are kept in fine-meshed nets for several days where they are fed finely mashed hard-boiled egg yolk and soybean milk (made by filtering finely ground soybean soaked in water). They are then transferred to small, shallow nursery ponds (1/3 meter deep). An ideal nursery pond has an ample supply of natural food and very few predatory insects. Organic fertilizers, including green compost or the roots and leaves of legumes, are applied to the nursery pond during the preparation period to encourage the growth of large quantities of protozoans, small crustaceans, and rotifers, which serve as food for the young fry. Unfortunately, many predatory insects are also attracted to a well-fertilized pond, where they lay their eggs. Among these insects, the water boatman, dragonfly, and backswimmer are particularly harmful; a single water boatman can attack and kill at least 4-5 fry a day. If a large swarm of insects manages to get into the pond, insecticides cannot be used for they will kill the fragile fry before the insects. A simple method is popularly used to control air-breathing predatory insects that must come to the surface to respire. An oil emulsion is prepared by mixing plant oil (usually unrefined coconut oil) with real soap (not detergent). This emulsion is diluted and sprayed onto the water. Insects surfacing to breathe cannot penetrate this film and suffocate or become entangled in the sticky substance and die, while fish fry remain unharmed.

When the fry have been in the nursery pond for about 10 days, they can be transported to local fingerling ponds or sold to farmers in other countries. The fry are usually conditioned before they are packed for shipment. This is done by taking a very fine net and drawing it from one side of the nursery pond to the other, concentrating the fry in a small area of the pond. They are left in this crowded condition for 5-6 minutes and then released. This procedure is repeated once a day for about 3 days to accustom the fry to being crowded.

Unconditioned fry and fingerlings frequently die of shock when suddenly packed in high densities.

After the third day the fish are collected and put into a net-box, suspended in a trough of slowly running water, for 5-6 hours, without feeding. Here they are allowed to void any waste material accumulated in their guts. Well-fed fry and fingerlings with full intestines and stomachs are not only extremely susceptible to injury, but may release wastes into the packing water, rapidly depleting its oxygen content. For short journeys the fry are transported in shallow open containers; mechanical agitation keeps the water well-aerated. Plastic bags inflated with oxygen are used to transport the fish for long distances. In hot weather ice is added to the bags. The fish conditioning and training periods have greatly decreased mortalities experienced in transporting fingerlings and fry, especially for long distances.

Fry are frequently kept in fingerling ponds two weeks or longer before they are stocked in the grow-out ponds. Fingerling ponds are organically fertilized to produce food for the fry. Natural pond food is often supplemented with foods such as soybean milk, soybean cake, wheat flour, and rice bran. Grass carp begin to show their preference for plant material in the fingerling stage. They are given *Wolfia,* (a small delicate plant closely related to duckweed), or if it cannot be found, finely chopped duckweed or tender aquatic algae. Gradually the grass carp fingerlings are introduced to the chopped tender leaves and stems of aquatic plants. By the time the fish are 6 inches long, they are feeding on the leaves and the stems of some suitable land grasses and land vegetations. Fingerlings are transported to grow-out ponds in the same way fry are transported (see above).

Ponds

A grow-out pond in the polyculture system may be anywhere in size from 0.1 hectare to larger than 10 hectares, depending on the type of polyculture involved. Intensive polyculture is practiced in small ponds (0.5-2 hectares) stocked with high densities of fish. Extensive culture involves stocking lower densities of fish in large bodies of water, at least 5-20 hectares in size. Intensive culture requires heavy application of fertilizers, ample supplementary feeding, and detailed management, while there is virtually no way the large bodies of water used in extensive polyculture can be effectively fertilized. Many of these are community-owned water reservoirs simultaneously being used for irrigation and other purposes.

Intensive polyculture ponds are the ones most commonly found in Southeast Asia; and the following discussion reviews techniques used in farming such ponds. Many are managed by individual families. One-half to 2 hectares seems to be the easiest size to manage. A large fish farm is often divided into a number of smaller units about 1-2 hectares in size, interconnected with a good main water supply, drainage system, and feeder canals. If the ponds are too small (less than 0.2 hectare), there is a dangerous tendency to stock more fish than the pond can support. During the summer, evaporation causes smaller ponds to dry up rapidly, and any leaks will drain water at a proportionately faster rate in a smaller pond.

As in all Southeast Asian fish ponds, a good polyculture fish pond is provided with water inlets and outlets at correct locations for efficient maintenance and control of water flow and level. The inlets are provided with fine-meshed screen to prevent the entry of fry and eggs of undesirable fish species, especially in areas where tilapia are a problem. The outlets are properly screened to prevent the escape of any cultured fish, especially if they have a tendency to migrate when they reach a certain size. The bottom of the pond often slopes gently from the water inlet towards the outlet. Near the outlet sluice gate is a small deep area similar to a sump pit. At the end of the culturing period, when the pond is drained for a total harvest, all fish can be driven into this sump pit. Larger ponds may also have trenches about 1-2 meters wide and 30-40 meters long, extending along the pond edges, to serve as additional fish collecting areas.

Prior to stocking, the polyculture fish pond is prepared using the same procedures described for milkfish culture: the pond is drained and dried, and fertilizers (either organic, chemical, or both) are applied. Many of the fish used in polyculture systems are hardy, and can survive through the winter without the aid of a wintering pond even in Taiwan. They can be introduced into a fresh pond by the end of February (compared to early April for milkfish).

Stocking Methods

In polyculture, each of the different species of fish used can be stocked in one or more sizes, depending on: (1) the quantity and type of food organisms available in the pond, (2) the amount of time and money the owner is willing to invest until harvest time, (3) market conditions, (4) the availability of young fish of the proper stocking size, and (5) availability and cost of suitable supplemental feed. Each fish farmer is guided by his own experience, skill, and preferences. An experienced fish farmer well acquainted with a pond is able to make a surprisingly accurate prediction of the fish production capacity of that pond. Such predictions frequently become production targets. A mortality rate of 15-20% before harvest time is usually taken into consideration when stocking numbers are calculated.

Feed

The fish used in Southeast Asian polyculture ponds feed best at temperatures around 20-30°C; if the temperature drops below 15°C, feeding activity is drastically reduced. Below 10°C most of the fish cease feeding. During the winter in Taiwan, the fish are fed when the water warms slightly around noon.

If a pond is well fertilized, only a small amount of supplemental feeding is usually necessary. Grass carp alone must be fed since they frequently consume all the aquatic weeds in a pond within 2-3 months. Any soft and tender aquatic plants or land grasses, such as alfalfa leaves, elephant grass, the discarded outer coverings of vegetables such as cabbage, and the leaves of sweet potatoes, beans, tapioca, and legumes, are suitable as feed. This material must be concentrated in one area of the pond and the fish must be trained to eat there daily. If this is not done, excess material often sinks to the bottom of the pond to rot. A triangular or square floating "feeding ring" made of three or four bamboo poles is anchored to a pole at one end of the pond, not far from the bund. The grass carp are fed here twice a day.

When grass carp are given feed, the production of other fish in the pond system is also increased. The grass carp greedily ingests large quantities of plant material, rapidly passing them through its digestive tract. The cellulose is broken down, but the potentially digestible material is only partially utilized. Grass carp droppings contain a considerable amount of nutrition, and are often consumed by the silver, bighead, and common carp, which further utilize the partially digested material. Droppings that are not consumed directly by other fish serve as fertilizer at the bottom of the pond.

Unfortunately, grass carp will not eat some of the most troublesome aquatic plants such as: water hyacinth (*Eichhornia* spp.), water lettuce (*Pistia* sp.) or rabbit ear (*Salvinia* sp.) unless they are starving; these plants are too coarse for them. These troublesome plants can multiply to cover an entire pond surface

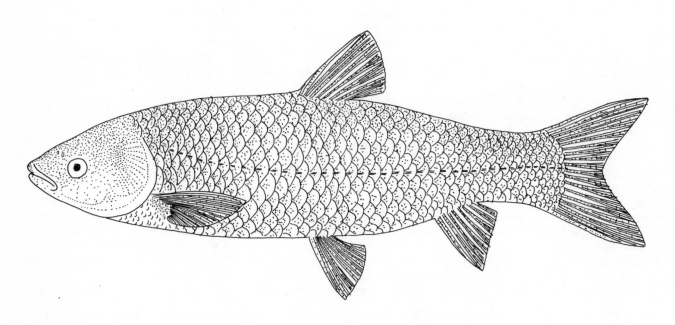

ILLUSTRATION 5.   Grass carp   *Ctenopharyngodon idellus* (Cuvier and Valenciennes) (After H. C. Yang)

within 1-2 months in a warm climate, making the pond habitable for only a few air-breathing fish, such as *Clarias* catfish or snakeheads. Fish farmers must remove this vegetation by hand.

Harvesting

When multiple-size group stocking has been performed in a polyculture pond, the first crop of fish can be harvested within 2-3 months. Harvesting is repeated about every 2 months thereafter; following each harvest a new batch of small fish is stocked. The process is the same as that described for milkfish except the operation here deals with four to five kinds of fish rather than one. The timing of harvesting is carefully planned to coincide with market demands, especially periods of major festivities when fish are readily sold at a high price.

Culturing operations are continued in a pond until a large quantity of organic material has accumulated at the bottom, generating poisonous gases and using up oxygen. Under these conditions, especially during a hot summer when sudden heavy cold rain may fall after a few windless cloudy days, the danger of sudden massive fish kills is great. These fish kills are brought about primarily by depletion of oxygen and the effects of "upwelling" of the pond bottom. Windless cloudy days reduce photosynthetic action of aquatic plants and thus decrease generation of oxygen. Torrential summer showers suddenly cool the surface layer of the pond; warm water at the bottom rises as the cool rain water from above digs down into the bottom, and within a few hours the pond bottom is turned upside down. Accumulated gases, such as sulfur dioxide and methane, as well as decaying organic material, are churned up and dispersed throughout the pond; the oxygen content of the water is reduced to virtually zero. A good fish farmer always watches his pond carefully. If there is any sign that the fish are suffering from lack of oxygen, or if after a few continuous quiet cloudy days it appears that there may be a heavy rain and the pond is "old," he either starts his pumps recirculating and spraying water over the pond, introduces fresh water from a nearby creek or canal, or mechanically agitates and aerates the water. The cause and effect of the upwelling phenomenon are still not completely understood. Simple but effective ways to prevent such upwelling are introduction of fresh water or vigorous agitation and recirculation of water before upwelling starts.

Table 16 gives rough estimates of the cost and profit of an average 1-hectare polyculture fish pond in Taiwan. According to these rough estimates, the net profit per hectare of pond is about NT $24,000, or US $600. Since many of these farms are managed by the fish culturist, the wages for labor are paid to himself. The fish culturist in Southeast Asia usually does not spend all his time managing the pond, but also engages in some other work.

The figures given in Tables 17 and 18 are based on data collected several years ago in close cooperation with fish farmers. It is important to realize that it is extremely difficult to obtain quantitative data concerning Southeast Asian fish ponds. Fish farmers seldom keep records of operation and production, and the few who do are rarely willing to give out accurate information.

Tables 17 and 18 display some of the major differences between production in an intensive (heavily fertilized pond) and extensive (unfertilized farm reservoir) polyculture system. These differences are reflected in the quantities and types of potential food organisms available, and consequently, the composition of fish populations harvested from each of the impoundments. We should keep in mind that some of the purposes for which intensive and extensive polyculture systems are farmed are frequently not quite the same. A heavily fertilized fish pond is managed by a farmer seeking to make as much profit, and therefore produce as many fish, as possible. A reservoir or community water supply is usually managed to satisfy a number of different goals; the production of fish is just one of them.

We can see from Table 17 that the fertilized pond produces ten times the amount of phytoplankton and zooplankton produced in the unfertilized reservoir, as

TABLE 16.

PROJECTED ANNUAL PROFIT AND LOSS STATEMENT FOR A 1-HECTARE POLYCULTURE FISH POND (Taiwan, 1974)

	NT (New Taiwan dollar)[A]
REVENUE	
Sale of fish (3,500 kg at NT $24/kg)	$84,000
EXPENDITURES	
Interest on capital investment (10%)	NT $10,000
Amortization of principal structures (10-year period)	2,000
Equipment	1,000
Maintenance and repair	2,000
Stocking material (fingerlings)	6,000
Feeds and fertilizers	25,000
Wages (labor- 1/3 person)	12,000
Miscellaneous	2,000
TOTAL PRODUCTION EXPENDITURES	$60,000
NET INCOME	NT $24,00 or US $600

Source: Ling's estimate.
A. New Taiwan dollar (NT $40 = US $1).

well as greater quantities of benthos and nekton. However, the fertilized pond produces fewer macrophytes (higher plants) than the reservoir. This is due to the fact that the swarms of plankton in a heavily fertilized pond reduce the amount of light penetrating to the macrophytes, hindering their growth.

The species and numbers of fish harvested from each of the impoundments (Table 18) reflect the differences in quantities and types of food organisms listed in Table 17. As expected, the percentage of macrophyte-eaters harvested from the farm reservoir is significantly higher than that obtained from the fertilized pond. Total weight of fish harvested from the heavily fertilized pond exceeds 7,000 kilograms/hectare/year, while the unfertilized reservoir produces only one-sixteenth of that amount. Actually, an unfertilized pond that is well managed and well stocked can produce up to 500-600 kg fish/ha/year. The low production in the farm reservoir (400 kg/year) is probably due to the widely fluctuating water levels induced by irrigation practices (the primary purpose of a farm water reservoir is irrigation of ricefields).

Looking again at the standing crop figures of food organisms available in the fertilized pond (Table 17), we can roughly calculate that the pond should be able to support 4,000 kg of fish. Yet the production figure given is 7,000 kg. The remaining 3,000 kilograms of fish are produced by direct utilization of fertilizer. In some heavily fertilized ponds, half of the fertilizer goes into production of food organisms while the other half serves directly as feed. It is possible to reduce the amount of fertilizer used and replace it with supplemental feed to produce the same quantity of fish. Relative costs of organic fertilizers and supplemental feeds are factors used in deciding how much of each category to use for the best economic return.

Table 19 lists the organic fertilizers used in polyculture fish ponds in Southeast Asia. Amounts of crucial

TABLE 17.

ANNUAL WET WEIGHT PRODUCTION AND Eβ VALUES OF STANDING CROPS OF BIOTIC CONSTITUENTS IN TWO TYPES OF IMPOUNDMENTS (Taiwan, 1970)

| | HEAVILY FERTILIZED FISH POND | | UNFERTILIZED FARM WATER RESERVOIR | |
	Wet weight (kilograms/hectare)	Eβ value[A]	Wet weight (kilograms/hectare)	Eβ value[A]
Phytoplankton	6,772	86.4	654	54.6
Zooplankton	492	6.3	48	4.0
Macrophytes	117	1.5	377	32.0
Zoobenthos	362	4.7	77	6.5
Nekton	86	1.1	34	2.9
Total biota	7,829	100.0	1,190	100.0
Total plankton	7,264	92.7	702	58.6
Total plants	6,889	87.9	1,031	86.6
Total animals	940	12.1	159	13.4

Source: Y.A. Tang, 1970.
A. Eβ value = weight percentage of a particular biotic group of the total biota.

chemical elements (nitrogen, phosphorus, and potassium), are given for each fertilizer. In newly constructed Southeast Asian fish ponds, nitrogen is usually the limiting factor. In well-seasoned ponds there is a surplus of nitrogen, and phosphorus appears to be the needed plant nutrient. Theoretically, it seems possible to replace organic fertilizers with inorganic fertilizers mixed in the appropriate ratios. Experiments have been conducted using inorganic chemicals as the sole fertilization in a pond. Results were not quite as good; plankton produced by this method was not as rich or abundant as that grown with organic fertilizers. The presence of some "trace" substances found in organic fertilizers is thought to be necessary. When organic and inorganic fertilizers were combined, results were excellent.

Unfortunately, inorganic fertilizers are often too costly for the fish farmers of Southeast Asia to use. A major drawback to cheap, effective organic manuring is the problem of disease. Although night soil is thoroughly disinfected before use, heavy infestations of certain kinds of human parasites frequently occur in fish culture areas. Some of these parasites have aquatic intermediate hosts, such as *Cyclops* (a copepod), snails, or fish, and may release their infective stages directly into the water. People working in the ponds without proper protection come into contact with these infective young stages, such as the circariae of blood flukes, which bore through the epidermis of the victim to enter his circulatory system. The problem of intestinal parasitic infection is especially serious in children. Liver fluke cysts are present in fish muscle in certain areas of Southeast Asia; these can infect the consumer if the fish is eaten half-cooked or raw, a common practice in that part of the world. The prevention and control of these problems are dealt with by health officers in close cooperation with fish culturists. The fish farmer takes proper control measures as advised by the health officers, especially if parasites are detected in the area. People are warned not to eat raw or half-cooked fish produced in an infected area.

TABLE 18.

SPECIES COMPOSITION OF FISH POPULATIONS HARVESTED FROM TWO TYPES OF IMPOUNDMENTS (1 year)

Species	HEAVILY FERTILIZED FISH POND		UNFERTILIZED FARM WATER RESERVOIR	
	Species weight (kilograms/hectare)	E_β value[A]	Species weight (kilograms/hectare)	E_β value[A]
Silver carp	2,706	37.1	262	61.8
Bighead carp	736	10.1	25	5.9
Grass carp	263	3.6	73	17.2
Grey mullet	2,502	34.4	17	4.0
Common carp	910	12.5	28	6.6
Black carp			6	1.4
Sea perch	170	2.3	13	3.1
TOTAL	7,287	100.0	424	100.0
Species feeding on plants (silver carp, grass carp, grey mullet)	5,471	75.1	352	83.0
Species feeding on animals (bighead carp, common carp, black carp, sea perch)	1,816	24.9	72	17.0
Plankton feeders (silver carp, bighead carp, grey mullet)	5,944	81.6	304	71.7
Higher plant eaters (grass carp)	263	3.6	73	17.2
Benthic feeders (common carp, black carp)	910	12.5	34	8.0
Nekton feeders (sea perch)	170	2.3	13	3.1

Source: Y.A. Tang, 1970.

A. E_β value = weight percentage of a particular biotic group of the total biota.

TABLE 19.
ORGANIC MATERIAL COMMONLY USED AS FERTILIZER IN POLYCULTURE PONDS IN SOUTHEAST ASIA (1 year)

ORGANIC MATERIAL	TOTAL WEIGHT OF DRY MATTER (kilograms)	NUTRIENT COMPOSITION (kilograms)		
		NITROGEN	PHOSPHORUS	POTASSIUM
Rice bran	1,700	34	33	20
Chicken manure	1,300	19	13	8
Pig manure	1,200	14	6	5
Night soil[A]	8,400	200	144	120

A. Properly disinfected (cow manure is often used instead).

16 Combination Polyculture

Most of the Southeast Asian fish farmers are rural people, and profits gained from the culture of fish are often not sufficient to provide for their families. Rather than traveling far away to work, the culturists prefer to engage in additional activities close to home, preferably having some connection with the ongoing fish culture. The Southeast Asian people have thus developed many combinations and integrations of farming activities using fish polyculture as the mainstay.

The simplest type of integrated culture is the planting of useful aquatic vegetation in a corner of the pond. *Ipomoea* is commonly grown in Southeast Asian fish ponds. Its greens are used for human consumption like spinach or water cress, while its root system harbors epiphytes (algae, diatoms, small insects) that fish can feed on. Coarser stems are used to feed chickens, while roots may be used as compost. The clumps of plants serve as hiding places for small fish and provide shade during hot summer days.

Vegetable gardening is often done on the banks of a fish pond. Water from the pond is used to irrigate the vegetables. Mud from the pond bottom, rich in organic material, is used as fertilizer for the gardens. Conversely, the unused or uneaten parts of the vegetables are thrown into the pond as fish food or fertilizer.

Fruit trees may also be grown on the banks of ponds, especially in Indonesia, Malaysia, Singapore and Thailand, where coconuts, bananas, and papayas are often so-cultivated. In some fish farming centers of South China, thousands of acres of pond embankments and land between ponds are used for growing sugar cane. Since the pond requires morning sun (the earlier the sun's energy can get to the pond, the sooner the replenishment of oxygen by photosynthesizing plants within,) tall trees are not planted on the eastern banks of the ponds. They are grown on the western side, where they provide shade and help to keep the pond cool during the hottest period of the day.

Some fish ponds may have chicken coops along the banks; the chicken droppings are allowed to fall into the ponds as fertilizer. Pig sties may also be constructed alongside pond banks. Pond water is used to clean the pig sty, then flushed into a small holding reservoir for disinfection before being reintroduced into the pond as fertilizer. Enterprising families may have aquatic vegetation, vegetable gardens, fruit trees, chickens, pigs, and even cattle growing in conjunction with the fish pond.

When polyculture is done on a large scale, as by an entire village, it may be integrated with silk production. Silkworms hatch from eggs, then grow large feeding on mulberry leaves. They subsequently spin cocoons in which they are transformed into pupae that emerge from the cocoons as moths. Silk taken from the cocoons is spun into silk threads.

Mulberry trees require a great deal of water and fertilizer to grow well. In certain fish farming centers in China, large numbers of mulberry trees are grown on broad embankments between ponds. Organic material taken from the pond bottom during the period of pond preparation may be used as fertilizer for the mulberry trees.

Another fish polyculture combination system is the culture of fish in conjunction with ducks. Chickens are land animals and polyculture with them simply involves use of their droppings as fertilizer. Ducks spend a great deal of time in water and are far more useful in combination with fish polyculture. Both egg-laying ducks and those intended for table consumption may be reared with fish. The pond is separated into two areas with a partition made of wide-mesh wire screen that allows the fish but not ducks to pass through. A shed is built on the bank for the ducks, with separate compartments for young ducks, egg-layers, and ducklings. The ducks are usually fed material available cheaply from the local market such as corn, rice bran, fish meal, or trash fish. The ducks are fed heavily, and a great deal of money is spent buying them feed. In exchange, they discharge large amounts of excrement directly into the water, fertilizing the pond very efficiently. A few hundred ducks can produce enough fertilizer to adequately service an average-sized fish pond. Duck droppings are used either directly as food by the fish, or indirectly by supporting the growth of food organisms. Leftover duck feed may also be thrown into the pond as feed fertilizer.

A fish-duck pond is able to produce as many fish as any other polyculture fish pond of similar size without the use of any fertilizers other than those connected with duck raising (mentioned above). Average production of fish is about 3,500 kg/ha/year. Additional money can be made by selling the ducks and duck eggs. Duck-fish polyculture is an ancient practice that was badly neglected before World War II, revived again within the last ten years, and has spread rapidly. It is usually practiced in areas with poor rice-growing potential due to frequent flooding, high salinity caused by high tides, or typhoons.

17 Crustacean Culture

Three main groups of crustaceans are cultured in Southeast Asia—marine penaeid shrimps, freshwater prawns (*Macrobrachium rosenbergii* spp.), and crabs.

Marine Shrimp

Rearing of marine shrimps is being popularly done in Southeast Asia. Existing practices range from simple, traditional trapping-holding-growing ponds to modern, sophisticated techniques. Traditional methods are used extensively because they are simple, easy to practice, and well known. The modern techniques of complete shrimp husbandry have a history of less than 20 years, but are advancing rapidly.

Marine shrimp culture may be grouped into categories according to how the shrimp are stocked and in what kinds of ponds they are raised:

Natural stocking (shrimp enter naturally with water inflow)

Shrimp ponds—Singapore, Thailand, Vietnam, Malaysia, Indonesia, almost every country in the Southeast Asian region

Brackish-water milkfish ponds — Indonesia, the Philippines, Taiwan, Vietnam

Coastal paddyfields — many in Vietnam, some in Thailand

Controlled stocking

Shrimp seed collected from natural habitats and stocked in:

Shrimp ponds — Taiwan, the Philippines, Thailand, Indonesia

Brackish-water fish ponds — Philippines, Taiwan, Indonesia

Seed produced in hatcheries for stocking in shrimp or fish ponds

A recent development, found in Taiwan, the Philippines, Indonesia and Thailand (Taiwan is leading with the other three countries following in development of this system)

NATURAL STOCKING. Shrimp culture in Singapore is one of the best examples of the traditional Southeast Asian method of rearing naturally stocked shrimp in shrimp ponds. Shrimp ponds are constructed in coastal mangrove swampland a short distance from the seacoast along tidal canals. An average-sized shrimp pond covers about 15-20 hectares. Mangrove trees are first removed, then strong bunds are constructed around the cleared area to create an enclosure — a pond, with water gates leading into a tidal canal. Each water gate has a strong sluice in which wire net screens can be inserted. During high tide the water gates are opened and water flows freely into the pond. When the tide is at its height, the gate is closed and all that has entered the pond, usually a mixture of prawns and young fish, is trapped inside. This procedure is repeated for several days; then the screen is lowered permanently, allowing water to pass freely but keeping the trapped organisms within. The mangrove swamps of Singapore are rich in organic material, and shrimp ponds constructed on this fertile land are well able to produce large quantities of food organisms for both young shrimps and fish. Well provided with food, the young shrimps can reach market size within two months after their entry into the pond. Shrimp are harvested during the full and new moon periods, at the time of the spring tides. At the height of the tide a conical net is inserted into the sluice gate, replacing the screen. The full-grown shrimp, instinctively tending to leave the pond with outflowing water during the receding tide, are trapped in the net. Harvesting is continued for about one week during each spring tide period.

Since stocking is accomplished by a natural process and an abundant supply of food is naturally present in the pond, no cost is involved in stocking or feeding the shrimp. Principal expenses are incurred in construction and subsequent preparation and repair of the pond and its bunds and sluice gates, and perhaps for construction of a hut for the pond-keeper. This simple, traditional form of shrimp culture can produce 250-400 kg of shrimp/hectare/year; with the low cost of operation, the profit from a pond is enough to support a small family.

The main disadvantages of this traditional system of shrimp culture result from the lack of control the culturist has over the stocking process. Larval and young shrimp populations fluctuate unpredictably under natural conditions, and the farmer cannot predict or regulate the kinds or number of shrimp entering the pond. The uncontrolled entry of predatory or competitive species with the young shrimp keeps production down. There are at present about 300 hectares of shrimp ponds in Singapore. In Thailand, Indonesia, and Vietnam, thousands of hectares of shrimp ponds managed in this traditional way remain in active operation. These ponds have great potential for development as soon as shrimp hatcheries progress to the point where postlarvae of desired species of shrimp can be mass-produced. Farmers will be able to practice controlled stocking in the ponds, increasing shrimp production by at least one hundred percent.

Many brackish-water milkfish ponds are located in areas where they can be stocked with shrimp larvae and young shrimp by the same natural process described above. However, in milkfish ponds, milkfish production is the primary goal, and shrimp culture remains secondary. Shrimp production is correspondingly lower than that in shrimp ponds; average production in such a system is about 20-30 kg shrimp/hectare/year.

Paddyfield shrimp culture is very popular in Vietnam, where a long coastline harbors extensive ricefield acreage. Some of the paddyfields are so close to tidal land that they become flooded with sea water during certain periods of the year and cannot be used to grow rice. During this time, about 6 months out of the year, the fields are converted into shrimp ponds, stocked by the natural process described above, and managed in the same way as shrimp ponds are in Singapore or Thailand. Production in the fields at present is low, about 50-100 kg shrimp/ha/year. Nevertheless, these coastal paddyfields have tremendous potential to double or triple their present productivity when quality shrimp seed can be produced for controlled stocking.

CONTROLLED STOCKING. Some seed is collected from natural habitats. Two main groups of shrimp are collected and cultured using controlled stocking methods, *Penaeus* spp. and *Metapenaeus* spp. Pound for pound, the larger *Penaeus* is worth at least twice the price of the *Metapenaeus* and consequently is preferred for stocking by most culturists.

Shrimp seed of the cultured species are collected by professional seed collectors from estuarine areas, tidal canals, and mangrove areas using simple hand nets or tow nets. One type of net used extensively for shrimp seed collecting is conical; it tapers to an open end which is drawn through a float, leaving the open end above water. When the net is towed through the water, the young shrimps are not crushed (as they would be in a traditional, closed-end net), but collect at the water surface in the open end of the net. While one man tows the net, another follows behind with a basin, repeatedly scooping out shrimps from the net into the basin. After about an hour of collecting, the basin is brought to shore where the two main groups of shrimp seed are separated. Metapenaeid seed, small but active, are already shrimplike in appearance. The slender penaeid seed move sluggishly and resemble matchsticks. Penaeid seed, worth about NT $0.40 each, are sold individually; metapenaeid seed, worth only about NT $0.04 each, are sold by the cupful. Shrimp seed collecting is becoming more and more difficult. Most coastal waters have become polluted and many tidal canals are being modified for irrigation and navigation. Young shrimps have become more and more scarce.

Some shrimp seed is produced in hatcheries. About ten years ago, culturists began to experiment with artificial propagation of shrimp and production of shrimp seed under controlled conditions in hatcheries. However, techniques for rearing shrimps to maturity in ponds have not yet been developed. Occasionally, a specimen with ripe ovaries or testes is found in a pond, but the occurrences cannot be duplicated at will. At the present time, shrimp hatcheries must still rely on gravid female specimens obtained from natural habitats as a source of fertilized eggs.

Shrimp fishermen are taught how to recognize gravid, mated female shrimp and are provided with special, aerated containers in which to bring them back alive. It is not very difficult to recognize a sexually mature shrimp. A well-developed ovary is indicated by the presence of a broad, dark granular lobe along the dorsal median portion of the cephalothorax and abdomen, and can be seen by bending the shrimp and looking through the thin membrane between the cephalothorax and abdomen. However, the presence of a ripe ovary does not necessarily mean that the shrimp has already mated and that her eggs will be fertilized when ovulated.

All female penaeid shrimp have a thelycum, located on the ventral side of the cephalothorax between the fourth and fifth pair of walking legs. Different species are characterized by thelycums of different sizes and shapes. The first pair of swimmerets of a mature male shrimp carries a flaplike structure called a petasma. During the process of mating, the petasma of the male transfers and deposits a sperm-bearing spermatophore into the seminal receptacle of the female, beneath the thelycum, followed by a stopper to plug the receptacle. Prior to mating, the thelycum of a female shrimp is empty and flat; after mating it becomes full and convex because of the presence of the spermatophore. The translucent outer surface of the thelycum becomes hard, opaque, and even calcified in some cases after mating. Mated specimens of female shrimps whose thelycum is a single ungrooved, circular-shaped structure can be recognized by the distinctive presence of the stopper, a pair of winglike structures protruding from the top of the thelycum. In species of female penaeid shrimp with a grooved thelycum, a very thin fragile stopper, which usually disappears within a few hours, is inserted in the groove. Often the only trace of the stopper is the presence of some dark fibrous material in the groove of the thelycum or a patch of white substance at the top of the thelycum. When specimens are selected for spawning, it must be taken into consideration that unmated mature shrimps are able to spawn but the eggs will not be fertilized, and that some immature female shrimps known to have mated are unable to ovulate.

A gravid female penaeid shrimp normally spawns at night at water temperatures ranging from 24-28°C. Ovulation can be delayed by gradually lowering the temperature of the holding water to 15°C by the addition of ice. Spawning tanks may be any of a number of sizes, but strong aeration is essential. A healthy, fully matured, mated female shrimp placed in a well-aerated, warm tank in the afternoon usually will spawn that very night. During spawning the female shrimp swims vigorously off the tank bottom, extruding 200,000 to 500,000 small eggs like a cloud, into the water. The newly released eggs are irregular in shape and covered with a thin layer of gelatinous substance which soon detaches to float to the surface of the water, giving it a foamy appearance and a distinctive odor. As soon as the gelatinous substance is removed, the eggs begin sinking and aeration is necessary to keep them afloat. Sinking eggs clump together, and those in the center will eventually suffocate.

Almost all species of penaeid shrimp that are being cultured have a more or less similar life history. At 24-28°C the eggs develop rapidly, and nauplii hatch out in about 14 hours. These nauplii do not feed, but subsist on yolk material. After molting six times, the nauplii become zoea, which begin to feed on phytoplankton. Penaeid zoea are usually fed mixed cultures of planktonic diatoms; an important component of the diet is *Skeletonema*. Any diatoms with long, hairlike setae are avoided, for larvae tend to become entangled in them and die. The zoea are carefully watched; if they carry long, threadlike feces, it is a good indication that they are feeding well and are healthy. Zoea molt three times to become myses (singular "mysis").

Some of the penaeid myses begin to feed on zooplankton immediately, while others change to zooplankton feeding more gradually; some penaeid myses feed on both phytoplankton and zooplankton throughout the mysis stage. *Artemia* (brine shrimp) nauplii, rotifers, veliger larvae, annelid and echinoderm larvae, or any kind of invertebrate larvae that is easily obtainable, are used as zooplankton feed. Myses are active swimmers, always swimming in a vertical position with their heads down. They molt three times to transform into postlarvae in about 5 days.

The various postlarval stages are indicated by a PL followed by a subscript indicating their age in days. Early stage postlarvae swim actively as do the mysids, but later stages become demersal. While in myses the thoracic legs are used for swimming; in postlarvae they have developed for clinging and holding, and the swimmerets are used for swimming. The penaeid postlarvae soon begin enlarging their diet. Some, such as *Penaeus japonicus*, feed entirely on food of animal origin; others like the postlarvae of *P. monodon*, feed on material of both plant and animal origin. (For this reason, *Penaeus monodon* is considered more convenient and cheaper to culture.) Small pieces of worms, clams, oysters, squid, fish, or other shrimp flesh are fed to the postlarvae as animal feed.

When the postlarvae are 20 days old (PL_{20}), they are ready for stocking into shrimp ponds. Some shrimp farmers prefer to stock PL_{30}, in which case the PL_{20} larvae are first transferred to a nursery pond before being introduced into the grow-out pond.

As of now, there is no standardized formula defining the density of postlarval stocking per unit area of pond. However, the popular stocking rate is rather low, being only 2-3 postlarvae per square meter of pond bottom area.

Shrimps cultured in ponds are very sensitive to sudden changes in water conditions such as oxygen depletion, increase in water pollutants, or the presence of decaying organic material on the pond bottom, especially when the population density is high. With low intensity stocking, the survival rate of the shrimp is usually much higher, especially when shrimp farmers are not acquainted with efficient methods of pond management and water quality control. A low stocking rate of 2-3 postlarvae per square meter results in the production of 400-500 kg of shrimp per crop/hectare. Six months are usually required to produce a marketable crop of shrimp (30 grams each) from young postlarvae. In many Southeast Asian countries, two crops of shrimp can be cultured per year, resulting in an annual yield of 800-1000 kilograms of shrimp per hectare. This production of shrimp, by weight, is less than that obtained in many forms of fish culture. However, the selling price of shrimp is at least three times that of fish, and this has induced more and more people to take an interest in penaeid shrimp culture.

Penaeus monodon is one of the most important shrimp in Southeast Asia, and has become increasingly popular in shrimp culture operations. It grows rapidly to a large size, feeds on both plant and animal material, and does not require a clean sandy bottom (as does *P. japonicus*). It can tolerate the presence of some organic substances on muddy bottoms, thrives in a wide range of water salinities ($10°$/oo to $38°$/oo), survives in ponds between rainy and dry seasons, and can withstand water temperatures ranging from $20°C$ to $35°C$. Other important species suitable for farming in this region include: *P. merguiensis*, *P. indicus*, *P. japonicus*, *P. semisulcatus*, and *Metapenaeus monoceros*.

Freshwater Prawns (*Macrobrachium* spp.)

SOME HISTORICAL NOTES. Modern freshwater prawn culture has a developmental history of less than 15 years, but has already generated world interest. Research and development projects have been initiated in most countries in Southeast Asia.

For a number of years, experiments on the rearing of prawn larvae, conducted by fishery biologists/aquaculturists all over the world, were unsuccessful. In 1961, a major breakthrough was successfully achieved at the Marine Fisheries Research Institute, Penang, Malaysia, when it was discovered that a certain amount of salinity was an important basic requirement for the survival, growth, and development of the larval stages of *Macrobrachium rosenbergii*. This discovery quickly led to other breakthroughs in the studies of food and environmental requirements of the larvae; the techniques for rearing hatchlings through all their larval stages were successfully completed and the first laboratory-reared juvenile prawn was produced in June 1962. Techniques for spawning and other hatchery operations were soon developed, and in the spring of 1963, sufficient numbers of juveniles were produced for conducting grow-out experiments in ponds. The results of the grow-out experiments were very encouraging, and news of these achievements spread rapidly to other countries.

I would like to share with you some of my experience in developing this new field of aquaculture. Among the many hundred failures and some successes experienced, those that are related to the problems of reproduction, larval survival, and larval food and feeding deserve special mention.

PROBLEMS CONCERNING REPRODUCTION—MATING AND BREEDING. To have egg-bearing females accessible at all times, we had to be able to mate and spawn the prawns. I tried to apply the knowledge and experience we had in spawning fish under controlled conditions to mating prawns. I carefully selected one nice-looking female prawn and one handsome male prawn, and put them together in a well-aerated aquarium. The next morning the male seemed happy, but part of the female's head was gone. I repeated this process with other pairs of prawns; usually the female would have various parts of the head and/or some of its appendages missing, eaten by the male. In some cases the entire female disappeared. One day I happened to repeat the experiment during the day, and while I watched, the female molted. I was concerned; now that the female's whole body was soft, the male would surely chew her up in a few minutes! By the time I had found a hand net, about 5 minutes later, I rushed back, hoping to be in time to rescue the female. To my surprise, instead of attacking the newly molted female, the male proceeded to lock the female in a protective embrace. When her new shell was hardened, they mated. The fact became apparent that mature male prawns are ready to mate anytime, but mature females require a premating molt. Before the premating molt, a mature female prawn is not responsive to the courtship of the male. Apparently the male prawn does not understand this, so when a healthy anxious male fails to get a response from a mature but unmated female, he feels humiliated and becomes angry enough to attack her. I had learned an important lesson. When one is working with prawns, one must think like a prawn. I had failed because all the time I had been thinking like a human being!

After discovering the simple facts of life of the prawns, we could now spawn them under controlled conditions, either by individual pairs or in large groups. For spawning individual pairs, the males and females were first separated. When a female molted, a male was put into the same tank, and the pair would always mate. If several females are put together in a tank and one molts, the others will attack her. However, when a female prawn molts in the presence of a male, she secretes certain chemicals that attract the male; before other females can attack, the male quickly embraces and protects her.

PROBLEMS OF LARVAL SURVIVAL. When I had obtained a gravid female prawn, I put it into a well-aerated tank full of clean water and observed the color of the eggs gradually change from orange to grey to slate grey, to black when the larvae hatched. A full tank of larvae! I thought that I had solved the whole problem. But within 6 days all the larvae had died. I obtained more larvae and subjected them to different concentrations of dissolved oxygen. They too died within 6 days. I tried again, varying the alkalinity, pH, temperature, everything I could think of. Nothing worked. These failures continued repeatedly many many times for over a year. Every 1-2 weeks I obtained a few new gravid females and hatched fresh batches of larvae, but none of the resulting several million hatchlings ever survived more than one week, and none of them ever developed to the second larval stage. I was strongly urged by colleagues, friends, and relatives to discontinue the research. But I was really obsessed, refused to give up, and obtained permission to continue. Many more failures later I got so desperate, thinking, "Well, they're going to die anyway, I might as well help them go more quickly," that I added such things as hay infusion, vegetable juice, tea, milk, sugar, salt, soil, coffee, soy sauce, fruit juice, etc. etc. to the larval culture containers. Lo and behold, some larvae in the rearing containers to which salt or soy sauce had been added survived to develop into second stage larvae. I had been so foolish! The simple fact is that the larval stages need dilute sea water for survival and development. It is not uncommon for different stages in the life cycle of some aquatic organisms to change from sea water to fresh water or vice versa. Since we had collected all the gravid prawns from fresh water, sometimes up to 100 miles away from the sea, we had been misled.

Similar experiments conducted by other fisheries biologists during the past 40 years had also failed because of the same mistake. We had regarded *M. rosenbergii* as a freshwater prawn, and had given the newly hatched larvae fresh water of the finest quality. For the first 5 days, the larvae bear yolk and can survive in fresh water. But when the yolk is exhausted, they must reach a slightly saline area to survive. Under natural conditions, larvae are hatched out in rivers or areas where there is a water current fast enough to carry them to coastal areas within 4-5 days, even if they begin over a hundred miles from the sea. The larvae are so small, no one had noticed them floating downstream. In fact, there was no record of a second stage *M. rosenbergii* larvae anywhere. This simple discovery was the so-called major breakthrough that made all the other experiments dealing with *Macrobrachium* culture possible.

PROBLEMS CONCERNING LARVAL FOOD AND FEEDING. Our next problem was to determine what to feed the larvae. Several species of zooplankton and other organisms that the larval prawns consumed were identified. We tried feeding the prawn larvae *Artemia* (brine shrimp) nauplii, an organism commonly used to rear larvae and fry of many shrimp and fish species. It worked very well, but was not a complete solution because *Artemia* eggs are imported, and thus are difficult to obtain and very expensive. Locally available material suitable as food for the larvae had to be found. After many trials, it was finally discovered that small pieces of fish flesh, shrimp, clam, worm, and egg custard were very convenient to use, easily obtainable, and satisfactory as food for the prawn larvae. Egg custard is made by steaming scrambled hen eggs at a temperature (60-70°F) just high enough to coagulate the substance without destroying vitamins or proteins. This substance is mashed and passed through a strainer to produce food particles of any desired size. Vitamins and even antibiotics may be added to the egg before it is steamed. *Macrobrachium rosenbergii* larvae will not feed on tiny food particles less than one-tenth of their body length. On the other hand, when they are fed large particles, they continue to cling to them as the particles sink to the bottom, and eventually die there. Therefore food particles must be just large enough to attract the larvae but not large enough to drag them to the bottom.

With the knowledge gained from the above discoveries, it was easy to develop the technique, and complete the system necessary for rearing larvae of *M. rosenbergii* to juvenile and then to adult size. The first three years of our research were full of frustrations, but after that, progress was rapid. Now other problems arose. When people heard of our success, they all wanted to come and observe, and we became a tourist center. The visitors did not want to hear an assistant speak to them, they wanted to hear me. If they were important persons, they felt slighted if I didn't speak to them in person. Of course all this was good support and encouragement, but it took too much of our time. At that time news of our prawn research was still confined to Asia, where a plentiful supply of prawns was available in local waters and people were not as enthusiastic to pursue it. I cautioned those that wanted to try *M. rosenbergii* culture that it was not easy, that many problems remained unsolved, and a lot more work needed to be done to have it developed into a practical and economical industry. Gradually the news spread to other countries. Eight years ago a group in Hawaii asked for specimens and today Hawaii has become one of the most important centers of *Macrobrachium* culture.

Macrobrachium culture has now spread to the southern part of North America, Puerto Rico, and some South American countries. The prospects are good, but time and concerted efforts are urgently needed to solve basic problems and to refine existing cultural techniques before large-scale commercial prawn farming becomes feasible.

Current Status of Prawn Culture in Southeast Asia

Macrobrachium rosenbergii is the species used. Most of the Southeast Asian countries have their own native stock; Taiwan imports theirs from Thailand. Most of the prawn seeds used for culturing are produced in prawn hatcheries, but some are collected from their natural habitats at night when many juvenile and young prawns are present below dams.

Techniques for raising larvae from eggs to juveniles have been fairly well developed. Apart from government experimental stations, several private prawn hatcheries are already in active operation in Thailand, Taiwan, and Malaysia. The system used is only moderately modernized and leaves considerable room for improvement.

Principal problems in the rearing of larvae are: (1) difficulties in getting a sufficient supply of unpolluted sea water (this is becoming a major constraint in the development of commercial-scale production of prawn seeds); (2) maintenance of favorable water conditions; (3) food and feeding (The present trend is to minimize the use of Artemia, which are all imported and have become increasingly expensive and difficult to obtain. Locally available material found to be useful as larval food includes minute fish eggs, small pieces of animal and plant material such as aquatic worms, mussels, cockles, clams, squids, insect larvae, myses, *Acetes*, cheap crustaceans, fish, steamed egg custard, grains, beans, etc., and minute live food such as rotifers, *Cyclops*, copepods, daphnids and other entomostracans); and (4) prevention and control of high mortality of larvae.

Newly metamorphosed juveniles are usually allowed to remain in the larval tank for 1-2 weeks before transfer to juvenile tanks. Water in the juvenile tanks is maintained at very low salinity. Locally available material suitable as food for juveniles includes small pieces of fish, cheap shrimps, *Acetes*, chironomid larvae, aquatic earthworms, squids, mussels, grains, beans, and some kind of pellet forms of high protein fish feeds.

Most of the farming operations are still at an early stage of development and are conducted on a pilot-scale. Techniques used are basically those of existing Asian fish-farming methods: open earthponds, extensive in area, fairly labor-intensive, moderately mechanized, and involving little modern technology.

Most of the ponds used for prawn farming are converted from existing fish ponds; even new ponds are often constructed according to the traditional type of Asian fish ponds. They are earth ponds, rectangular in shape, 1,000-5,000 m² in size, 1-1.5 m in depth, and provided with an efficient water supply and drainage system. Fresh water is mainly used, but prawns also grow well in low-salinity brackish water.

Techniques used in Southeast Asia for preparing fish ponds include: (1) complete draining and drying of the pond (whenever possible); (2) levelling of the pond bottom, mending of the embankment, repair of water gates and water supply and drainage system; (3) application of lime and fertilizer; and (4) introduction of good fresh water into the pond.

Prawns may be stocked alone (monoculture) or together with nonpredatory fish (polyculture). To ensure good survival, juveniles 2-4 weeks old are used for stocking. When prawns are stocked with nonpredatory fish in a polyculture system, a stocking rate of 5,000-10,000/ha is generally used, and when cultured alone, about 15,000-30,000/ha.

In the present farming system, prawns depend a great deal on the food material produced in the pond. Supplemental feeds are given only in moderate amounts. Material used are trash fish or any nonoily inexpensive fish, small shrimps, mussels, squids, corn, peanut cake, soybean cake. Inexpensive fish and chicken feeds (pellets) are sometimes used.

Prawns are very sensitive to oxygen depletion. To minimize such danger, a gentle flow of water is maintained, especially at night. Whenever possible, ponds are provided with some aerators or water agitators. To help control excessive growth of aquatic plants and phytoplankton, a few grass carp and silver carp are stocked in the pond (when prawns are cultured alone).

There exists a wide range of rates of growth among the prawns; fast growers are able to reach marketable size within 3-4 months after being stocked, while others require much longer time. Partial harvesting with seine nets is often done at monthly intervals, to remove the large ones for the market and leave the small ones to continue growing. At the end of the culturing cycle, a complete harvest is done by draining the pond—sending large ones to market, and keeping small ones for the next stocking.

Crab Culture

The mangrove crab, *Scylla serrata*, is the only crab cultured to any great extent in Southeast Asia. The flavor and flesh of this crab are excellent, and in Asia and the Far East, the female crabs are prized for their ovaries. A mature female may cost up to three times more than a male crab or immature female. In Southeast Asia there are still no size regulations governing this crab fishery, a practice that will some day have to be initiated.

A small, young mangrove crab reaches maturity (market size) in 7-8 months. Spawning occurs throughout the year, especially in the warmer countries. Pollution seriously threatens natural production of the mangrove crab, and various culturing techniques have been experimented with. Unfortunately, there are major difficulties in rearing larvae from eggs to juvenile crabs. The larvae are extremely cannibalistic, and efficient, economical methods of rearing the larval stages to juvenile crabs have not yet been developed. Culturists have succeeded in mating the crabs and hatching the eggs, but only a few dozen crabs have survived from the initial million larvae. If we consider the wages and time spent, each of these crabs is worth at least $1,000. Academically, the research has met with a certain amount of success: the life history of the mangrove crab has been worked out. Economically, there are still many problems to be solved, and work is continuing on a small scale.

Many culturists in Hongkong, Taiwan, Thailand, and Singapore collect young, half-grown mangrove crabs from shallow coastal waters and mangrove swamps and stock them in ponds. Within 3-4 months these small, cheap crabs can be grown to market size. They are initially termed "lean" crabs, because they have little flesh.

In the ponds they are fed trash fish. When they have grown to market size, the mangrove crabs are separated by sex. The females are fattened with protein-rich food; within one month they develop ovaries, and can be sold for a much higher price. Prospects for development of this form of mangrove crab culture are good, especially along coastal mangrove flats where corrals can be built to grow lean crabs to market size.

Culture of the swimming crab, *Neptunus pelagicus*, is still in the early experimental stages.

18 Outlook for the Future

Some time has now been spent discussing the various aquaculture practices found in Southeast Asia. Aquaculture has been widely and popularly practiced in most of the countries there for many years. The fish, shrimp, and other aquaculture products of that region occupy a very important place in the diet of the people. From these lectures one might mistakenly think that there are very few problems in Southeast Asian aquaculture. Not so. Some problems are so overwhelming they are not even discussed.

Aquaculture as a whole is still an art. Most of the operations in Southeast Asia are done in an artistic way. An individual may have a successful farm, but someone else can hardly duplicate his methods to get the same results. It is like Chinese cooking—one can give the same recipe to five persons and very seldom will any two of them be able to produce a dish of similar quality. Even if one repeated a recipe, he could seldom produce the dish with identical quality a second time. To survive in this modern age of technology (i.e. to produce food on a large scale efficiently and economically) requires more than art alone. Fish culture in the Far East needs much concerted effort to catch up with modern technology.

Before World War II, every country in Southeast Asia had some form of fish culture. Many of these aquaculture operations were maintained in a traditional, empirical way, and little effort was made to improve or develop them. It was only after the war that fish culture was rediscovered as an excellent way to satisfy the growing demand for food.

Prior to World War II, most of the Southeast Asian countries we have discussed were not independent. Burma, Malaysia, Singapore, and Hongkong (which is still under the British wing) were British colonies. Indonesia was managed by the Dutch; Laos, Cambodia, and Vietnam were under French rule; and Taiwan was controlled by the Japanese. Thailand alone maintained her independence throughout this period.

The controlling powers were interested in getting as much as possible from their colonies, not in developing them for the benefit of the natives. Time, manpower, and money were spent on plantations (sugar, rubber, tea, coconut) whose products could be exported and sold for a large sum. Before each country gained its independence, the people had virtually no say in any developmental policy. Only after the second World War, when many of the Southeast Asian countries became self-governing, did they begin to develop fish culture. Unfortunately, there was still much unrest and fighting, and disturbances disrupted many programs. At present there are still troubles; in certain countries people dare not venture 10 miles from a city into the countryside.

Immediately after the war every country had many problems to solve, both domestic and foreign. Large sums of money were spent maintaining military and police forces. Fisheries programs were often given very low priority in national economic development plans and consequently received tiny budgets.

Each country in Southeast Asia is now struggling to develop its fisheries programs. One of the most difficult problems is the lack of able leadership and qualified fisheries personnel of all grades. People with potential for receiving higher education predominantly wanted to become medical doctors, engineers, or lawyers. Those few who entered fisheries schools usually shifted into other jobs after graduation since there were very few jobs in fisheries. They either joined the merchant marine, became biology teachers, or received scholarships to study abroad. Out of every ten persons who went to the United States for training, nine remained there. The small group of graduates who did return to their home countries were promoted to the rank of high officials, and no longer had the opportunity to do research or work with fish. What are needed most are good extension workers, those individuals who act as a liaison between the scientific personnel and the rural fish farmers. Unfortunately, extension workers are usually regarded as low-class technicians and receive low salaries.

In the few countries possessing enough technical personnel, technical aquaculture problems are similar to those here. One of the most important problems that remains to be solved is adequate supply of quality seed. This is often the bottleneck in the development of various types of aquaculture. Although induced spawning has been successfully performed on many important pond fish, basic studies are still needed. The life histo-ries, feeding habits, spawning habits, and fundamental physiology of many of the fish and shrimp being cultured today are still only vaguely understood. Another major problem is that of pond management, including the prevention and control of disease and parasites, and provision of an adequate supply of food for the cultured organisms. Traditionally, the color or smell of pond water was used to determine its quality, but these methods are not very reliable. There is a growing trend to analyze the water with more reliable equipment and then quantify how much fertilizer is needed, or how much energy should be used to create water circulation or provide air. Progress is coming, but very slowly. We

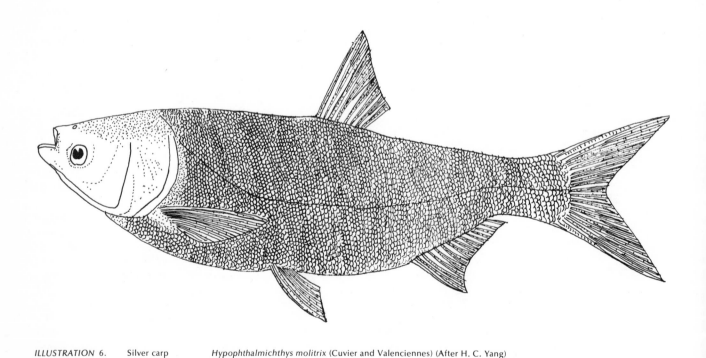

ILLUSTRATION 6.   Silver carp   *Hypophthalmichthys molitrix* (Cuvier and Valenciennes) (After H. C. Yang)

still don't understand many fundamental occurrences in polyculture systems. What is happening in the soil? How are the raw materials, organic and inorganic, changed into nutrients for primary productivity and into fish food? What complex interrelationships exist between the fish themselves, between fish and the environment, and between the environment and human activities? What presently unutilized species would do well in aquaculture systems?

Most importantly, each country must delineate a national policy for fish culture. So many things should be done, but where can a start be made? At present, unfortunately, very few Southeast Asian nations have drawn up well-defined fisheries development policies. There are many problems involved in being a newly independent country, trying to stand on its own two feet, with so much intended help from outside (technical assistance from United Nations agencies, bilateral agreements, the Peace Corps), sometimes aiding but often distracting. On what type of fish culture will the people of Southeast Asia place their emphasis: existing, traditional, labor-intensive practices, or modern methods using sophisticated technology and intensive mechanization? Changes are necessary, but how fast, and to what extent?

At the beginning of this book, I said, "If you give a fish to a person, you give him food for that day, but if you teach him to raise fish, then you help him to feed himself for the rest of his life." I think this philosophy applies not only to fish culture development, but to helping other countries in every way. We must give food to starving peoples in emergencies. But if we give food to them continuously, we will not be helping them—we will be turning those people into parasites. (Instead of just feeding the needy, we must train them to produce their own food.) To help people help themselves is most important, but also most difficult. As fish culturists we must not only solve our own production problems; we have obligations to help others with theirs. I will leave the reader with this as food for thought.

APPENDIX

Chinese Fish Culture[1]

By Fan Lee (5th Century B.C., China)

Translated by Ted S. Y. Koo, Chesapeake Biological Laboratory, University of Maryland, Solomons, Maryland 20688

Translator's note: "The Chinese Fish Culture Classic" was originally written by Fan Lee, a politician-turned fish culturist, in ancient China during the 5th Century B.C.

China has a long history of fish culturing. As long ago as the 12th Century B.C. there were fish rearing records in the Chinese Classics of early Chou dynasty (1112-221 B.C.). However, Fan Lee's work is the oldest known publication in Chinese literature on fish culture methods. Due to the antiquity of the article, some of the points mentioned in the text do not seem to make any sense. They are therefore not to be taken literally. For fear of second guessing the intent of the original author, however, this translator has tried the rendition rather literally. The purpose of this translation is merely to offer documentation of ancient Chinese fish culture work to Western literature and to give modern fish culturists some insight to the techniques of domesticating the common carp practiced nearly twenty-five hundred years ago.

King Wei of Chi[2], upon learning that Chu Kung was visiting in neighboring Tau, invited him over and asked: "I hear that you have been calling yourself a different name every time you visit a different country, and in Yuch you are called Fan Lee. Is it true?" "True," answered Chu Kung. The King continued, "You live in a very expensive house, and you have accumulated millions. What is the secret?" Whereupon Chu Kung responded: "There are five ways of making a living, the foremost of which is in aquatic husbandry, by which I mean fish culture. You construct a pond out of six mou[3] of land. In the pond you build nine islands. Place into the pond plenty of aquatic plants that are folded over several times. Then collect twenty gravid carp that are three chih[4] in length and four male carp that are also three chih in length. Introduce these carp into the pond during the early part of the second moon[5] of the year. Leave the water undisturbed, and the fish will spawn. During the fourth moon, introduce into the pond one turtle; during the sixth moon, two turtles; during the eighth moon, three turtles. The turtles are heavenly guards, guarding against the invasion of flying predators. When the fish swim round and round the nine islands without finding the end, they would feel as if they are in natural rivers and lakes. By the second moon of the next year, you can harvest 15,000 carp of one chih in length, 45,000 carp of two chih and 10,000 carp of three chih[6]. The total harvest can render a cash value of 1,-250,000 coins. The following year, you can get 100,000 carp of one chih, 50,000 carp of two chih, 50,000 carp of three chih, and 40,000 carp of four chih. Save 2,000 carp that are two chih in length as parent stock, and market the remainder. The take will amount to 5,150,000 coins. In one more year, the increase in income is countless."

Following the advice of Chu Kung, King Wei started a fish pond in his garden. In his first year, the King made more than 300,000 coins. In his pond, there were built nine islands. In addition, eight depressions were excavated. Each depression had two chih of water at the rim

1. Contribution No. 489. Chesapeake Biological Laboratory, University of Maryland, Solomons, Maryland, U.S.A.
2. Chi, a kingdom ruled by King Wei, 378-344 B.C.
3. Mou is a Chinese land measure of area. In today's standard, 6.6 mau equal one acre.
4. Chih is a Chinese measure of length. In today's standard, 1 chih is equal to 0.3581 meters, or 1.175 feet.
5. Chinese calendar goes by moon phases. Each moon of the year is 29 or 30 days. Generally it is approximately 1 to 1.5 months later than the Western calendar. The second moon is roughly equivalent to March; the fourth moon to May, etc.
6. The original versions have it as "15,000 carp of one chih in length, 45,000 carp of three chih, and 10,000 carp of two chih." I feel that this is a distinct error and have therefore changed the order to make better sense.

and six chih of water in the center. The carp would segregate themselves according to size in these depressions. The reason to raise carp rather than other species of fish is that the carp is not cannibalistic, that it is fast growing, and that it is inexpensive to raise.

Addendum[7]: Pond fish culture. Carp as large as three chih long are obtained only in the vicinity of large rivers and lakes. If you start with small fish, they would take too long to mature. If you start with the spawn, the method to collect spawn is to go to shore areas of rivers and lakes where large carp gather. Collect the mud at the water's edge, take a dozen loads or so and spread the mud on the bottom of the culture pond. Within two years there will be grown large carp. This is because the mud contains eggs of large carp, which hatch readily in pond water.[8]

7. The addendum section appears only in the Ching version but not in the Ming version.
8. Reprinted from *The American Fish Farmer* 3(8):10, by permission of Catfish Farmer and World Aquaculture News, Little Rock, Arkansas.

Glossary

agar. An extractive of red algae used as a gelling and stabilizing agent in foods.

alginic acid. A constituent of the cell walls of brown algae.

anaerobic. Conditions in which oxygen is absent and normal life that depends on oxygen is not possible.

anguillids. Belonging to the freshwater eel family.

barbel. A slender, tactile projection on the lips of certain fish.

benthic. Occurring at the bottom of a lake or sea.

benthos. All plants and animals living on the bottom of a lake or sea from shallow to great depths.

biota. Collective fauna and flora of a given region.

bund. An embankment constructed to contain water.

carrageenan. A seaweed extract used chiefly as a suspending agent in foods, pharmaceuticals, cosmetics, and industrial liquids; as a clarifying agent for beverages; and as an agent to control crystal growth in frozen confections.

cephalothorax. A body region formed by the fusion of one or more thoracic segments with the head, esp. in arachnids and crustaceans.

chironomids. Any of a very large family of minute, nonbiting midges, larvae, and pupae found primarily in fresh waters; adults often swarm in the evening.

ciliates. Protozoans having cilia or hairlike projections for locomotion and feeding—free-living or parasitic, marine or freshwater.

cloaca. The posterior common chamber into which the intestinal, urinary, and reproductive canals discharge.

copepods. Any of a large subclass of minute crustaceans common in fresh and salt water, having no carapace, 6 pairs of thoracic legs but none on the abdomen, and a single median eye.

Cyclops. Common genus of freshwater copepods.

daphnids. Primarily freshwater crustaceans of the genus *Daphnia*. Commonly called the "water flea," usually 0.5 to 3 mm long.

demersal. Living on or near the bottom of a lake or sea.

diatoms. Unicellular algae with walls impregnated with silica.

entomostracans. General taxonomic category of crustaceans including all the simpler forms such as copepods and daphnids, but excluding more advanced forms such as crab and shrimp.

epiphytes. Nonparasitic plants that grow on the surface of other plants.

eutrophication. Natural or artificial nutrient enrichment in a body of water, usually characterized by extensive plankton bloom and subsequent reduction of dissolved oxygen.

hectare. 10,000 square meters or 2.47 acres.

leptocephalus. The small, leaflike transparent planktonic larvae of the freshwater eel.

macrophyte. Any large aquatic plant.

mysis (pl. myses). Last free-swimming larval stage of some decapods, including shrimp, before metamorphosis to benthic postlarval form.

nauplius. Free-swimming, microscopic, first larval stage of many crustaceans, e.g. copepods, decapods, and barnacles among others.

nekton. Swimming marine and aquatic animals such as fishes and whales able to move about independently of currents.

petasma. A modfied branch of the first abdominal limb in a male decapod crustacean, used to transfer the spermatophore in the insemination process.

phytoplankton. All microscopic plants suspended in a marine or freshwater habitat. The plant component of plankton.

plankton. The passively drifting or weakly swimming organisms, both plant and animal, in marine or fresh water.

protozoans. Subkingdom comprising all unicellular organisms.

rotifers. Phylum of microscopic, primarily aquatic animals whose anterior end bears tufts of cilia used for feeding and locomotion.

somite. One of the longitudinal series of segments into which the body of many animals is divided.

spermatophore. A packet or capsule enclosing spermatozoa extruded by the male and conveyed to the female in the insemination of certain invertebrates.

suprabranchial. Above the gills.

swimmerets (pleopods). Appendages under the abdomens of many of the advanced crustaceans, used for swimming and/or creating oxygenating currents.

thelycum. Plates between the fourth and fifth walking legs in many female decapods making up the outer surface of the ventral pouch serving as a seminal receptacle.

zoea. One of several in a series of early larval stages (more advanced than the nauplius) of various decapods.

zooplankton. All animals suspended in the water of an aquatic habitat which are not independent of currents and water movements—most are microscopic; the animal component of plankton.

References

Bardach, John E., John Ryther, and W. O. McLarney. 1972. *Aquaculture—the farming and husbandry of freshwater and marine organisms.* Wiley-Interscience, John Wiley and Sons, Inc., New York.

Blanco, G. J. 1972. *Status and problems of coastal aquaculture in the Philippines.* Pages 60-67 *in* T. V. R. Pillay, ed. Coastal aquaculture in the Indo-Pacific region. West Byfleet, Fishing News (Books) Ltd., London.

Chen, T. P. P. 1952. *Milkfish culture in Taiwan.* Fish. Ser. Chin.-Am. Jt. Comm. Rural Reconstr. 1. 17 pp.

————1976. *Aquacultural practices in Taiwan.* Fishing News Books, Ltd., Surrey, England.

Delmendo, M. N. 1972. *The status of fish seed production in the Philippines.* Pages 208-212 *in* T. V. R. Pillay, ed. Coastal aquaculture in the Indo-Pacific region. West Byfleet, Fishing News (Books) Ltd., London.

FAO. 1967. *Proceedings of FAO Symposium on Warm-Water Pond Fish Culture.* FAO Fish. Rep. 44. 4 vols. FAO, Rome.

————1969. *Proceedings of World Scientific Conference on the Biology and Culture of Shrimps and Prawns.* FAO Fish. Rep. 57. 4 vols. FAO, Rome.

Ha Khao Chu, 1973. *Fisheries of Vietnam.* Southeast Asian Fisheries Development Center. SEAFDEC/SCS. 73:S-33. Singapore.

Hicklings, C. F. 1962. *Fish culture.* Faber and Faber, London.

Hora, S. L., and T. V. R. Pillay. 1962. *Handbook on fish culture in the Indo-Pacific region.* FAO Fish. Biol. Tech. Pap. 14. 203 pp.

Huet, Marcel. 1970. *Traite de pisciculture.* Editions ch. de Wyngaert. Bruxelles.

IDRC. 1973. *Problems of coastal aquaculture in Indonesia.* International Development Research Centre, Southeast Asia Aquaculture Seminar, Singapore. IDRC/AQS. 73 CP/18.

Le Van Dang. 1972. *Coastal aquaculture in Vietnam.* Pages 105-108 *in* T. V. R. Pillay, ed. Coastal aquaculture in the Indo-Pacific region. West Byfleet, Fishing News (Books)Ltd.; London.

Liao, I. C., and T. L. Huang. 1972. *Experiments on propagation and culture of prawns in Taiwan.* Pages 213-243 *in* T. V. R. Pillay, ed. *Coastal aquaculture in the Indo-Pacific region.* West Byfleet, Fishing News (Books) Ltd., London.

Lin, S. Y. 1966. *Milkfish farming in Taiwan.* Fish. Cult. Rep. Taiwan Fish. Res. Inst. 3:43-48.

Ling, S. W. 1957. *On the development of inland fisheries of Thailand.* FAO/ETAP Report to the Government of Thailand. FAO Rep. 653, FAO/57/6/4117. 50 pp.

————1965. *Production of fry and fingerlings of Chinese major carps by induced spawning.* FAO/ETAP Report to the Government of the Republic of China. FAO Rep. 2044. 12 pp.

————1965. *Development of inland fisheries, with special emphasis on fish culture.* FAO/ETAP Report to the Government of Malaysia. FAO Rep. 2095. 93 pp.

————1967. *Feeds and feeding of warm-water fishes in ponds in Asia and the Far East.* Pages 291-309 *in* Proceedings of FAO World Symposium on Warm-Water Pond Fish Culture FAO Fish Rep. 44, vol. 3.

————1969. *Role and possibilities of brackish water fish and shrimp farming in Southeast Asia.* Pages 352-360 *in* K. Tiews, ed. Proceedings of the International Seminar on Possibilities and Problems of Fisheries Development in Southeast Asia, organized by the German Foundation for Developing Countries, in cooperation with the Federal Board for Fisheries and FAO.

————1969a. *The general biology and development of Macrobrachium rosenbergii.* FAO Fish. Rep. 57, vol.3:589-606.

————1969b. *Methods of rearing and culturing Macrobrachium rosenbergii.* FAO Fish. Rep. 59, vol. 3:607-619

————1971. *Some brief notes on the status and problems of shrimp and prawn farming development in Asia.* Indo-Pacific Fisheries Council Meeting. IPFC/Exco/48/6. 14 pp.

————1972. *A review of the status and problems of coastal aquaculture of the IPFC region.* Pages 2-25 *in* T. V. R. Pillay, ed. Coastal aquaculture in the Indo-Pacific region. West By-fleet, Fishing News (Books) Ltd., London.

—————1973. *Status, potential, and development of coastal aquaculture in the countries bordering the South China Sea.* FAO/UNDP, South China Sea Fisheries Development and Coordinating Programme. SCS/DEV/73/5. 51 pp.

Medina, E., and R. O. Juliano. 1973. *Aquaculture problems in the Philippines,* Singapore, International Development Research Centre, IDRC Southeast Asia Aquaculture Seminar, IDRC-73, CP/15.

Ong Kah Sin. 1964. *The early development stages of* Scylla serrata, *reared in the laboratory.* Proc. Indo-Pac. Fish. Counc. 11(2):135-146.

—————1966. *Observations on the postlarval life history of* Scylla serrata *reared in the laboratory.* Malaysian Agric. J. —45(4).

Pathansali, D. 1961. *Cockle culture.* Proc. Indo-Pac. Fish. Counc. 11(11):84-98.

.Pillai, T. G. 1962. *Fish farming methods in the Philippines, Indonesia, and Hongkong.* FAO Fish. Biol. Tech. Pap. 18:1-68.

Pillay, T. V. R., editor. 1972. *Coastal aquaculture in the Indo-Pacific region.* West Byfleet, Fishing News (Books) Ltd., London.

Racek, A. A. 1972. *Indo-West Pacific Penaeid prawns of commercial importance.* Pages 152-172 *in* T. V. R. Pillay, ed. Coastal aquaculture in the Indo-Pacific region. West Byfleet, Fishing News (Books) Ltd., London.

Schuster, W. H. 1962. *Fish culture in brackish water ponds of Java.* Spec. Publ. Indo-Pac. Fish. Counc. 1. 143 pp.

Sidthimunka, Ariya. 1972. *Production of catfish* (Clarias *spp.*) *and its problems in Thailand.* Paper presented at the Seminar on the Problems of Innovating Agricultural Technology in Thailand, Ministry of Agriculture, Thailand.

Tang, Y. A. 1970. *Evaluation of balance between fish and available fish foods in multispecies fish culture pond in Taiwan.* Trans. Am. Fish. Soc. 99(4):708-718.

Tham, Ah Kow. 1968. *Prawn culture in Singapore.* FAO Fish Rep. 57, vol. 2:85-93.

Yang, Hung-chia, and Tung-pai Chen. 1971. *Common food fishes of Taiwan.* Chinese-American Joint Commission on Rural Reconstruction. Fisheries Series 10.